THE MUSLIM ST
   ORGANIZA.

Equal Opportunity

A collection of Muslim injustices in the American Education System

BY
ASAD GILANI
WITH
MEHREEN KHATEEB & MATEEN AMINYAR

EQUAL OPPURTUNITY

A Collection of Muslim Injustices in the American Education Sysytem

Copyright © 2022 By Asad Gilani

All rights reserved as permitted under the United States Copyright Act of 1976, no part of this publication may be reproduced, stored in a retrieval system, or transmitted in any form or by any means – electronic, mechanical, photocopying, recording, or otherwise – without the prior written permission of the publisher and copyright owners.

ACKNOWLEDGMENTS

Dean Aminyar
Rafael Espinal
Saira Gilani
Sophia Gilani
Zara Gilani
Ahmet Gundogdu
Alayna Khan
Farhat Khan
Khaja Khateeb
Muslim Students for Justice Organization

TABLE OF CONTENTS

INTRODCUTION	**1**
FOREWORD	**3**
CHAPTER 1: MUSLIM-TARGETED BULLYING IN THE EDUCATION SYSTEM	**7**
The Bullying of Muslims in the American Education System	9
Interview with Alayna Khan, Junior in High School	19
Interview with High School Bullying Specialist, Anonymous	23
The Day Everything Changed	27
A Short Story by Zara Gilani and Asad Gilani	27
Future Implications	37
Strength in Numbers	41
CHAPTER 2: THE LACK OF HALAL OPTIONS IN SCHOOL CAFATERIAS	**45**
The Lack of Halal Options in School Cafeterias	47
An Interview with New York City 37th District Former Councilman Rafael Espinal.	53
Rice Krispie Treat, Please!	59
CHAPTER 3: THE DETRIMENT OF EID NOT BEING ACKNOWLEDGED AS A SCHOOL HOLIDAY	**63**
The Detriment of Eid Not Being Acknowledged as a School Holiday	65
Interview with Khaja Khateeb, President of the NJ Eid Committee	71
Full 180	79

CHAPTER 4: THE NEGATIVE EFFECTS OF THE FLAWED P.E. AND SPORTS SYSTEM TOWARDS MUSLIM STUDENTS — 85

The Negative Effects of The Flawed P.E. and Sports System Towards Muslim Students — 87

Interview with Ahmet Gundogdu, 12th Grade Student and Varsity Tennis Player — 93

Reform, Never Tolerate — 99

FINAL REMARKS — 107

ABOUT THE ORGANIZATION — 109

Introduction

FOREWORD

By Sophia Gilani

Post September 11, 2001, life in the United States changed drastically for Muslim Americans. The war on terrorism also created a war for Muslims: the long and uphill battle against Islamophobia. Anti-muslim hate crimes, racial profiling, and faith-based discrimination all sharply increased post 9/11, creating an extensive and detrimental feeling of alienation for Muslim-Americans nationally.

The United States boasts one of the most superior education systems in the world. Such a title, however, often leaves a lack of room for scrutiny. While the U.S. education system is one to look up to, it is also one riddled with injustice and inequality. Muslim-American students have long battled with a school system lacking in accommodations for their religious practices: a lack of halal options in cafeterias, restrictive school athletics, and physical education policies, and an unwillingness to acknowledge Muslim holidays in the academic calendar. Post 9/11 brought along with it a new form of alienation for Muslim students: stares felt by peers when terrorism was discussed, which quickly turned into bullying and isolation for these targeted students.

In *Equal Opportunity,* the Muslim Students For Justice Organization aims to shed light on the injustices Muslim-American students face in the U.S. public school system. Written entirely by Muslim-American students (with the aid and input of Muslim peers, community members, school officials, and lawmakers alike), this work pushes readers to rethink their perception and understanding of the U.S. education systems, and whether or not the anti-discrimination policies they boast are as effective in practice as they claim to be.

—

The Muslim-American student experience is not one without difficulty. For most, it comes with a constant reminder that the school system was not created with all religious identities in mind. Cafeterias do not accommodate Muslims who eat in accordance with halal guidelines, in which certain foods and meats cannot be consumed. Athletic departments do not accommodate Muslim athletes who cannot wear shorts, skirts, tank tops, and other athletic attire when they participate in sports. Physical education curricula do not accommodate Muslim students who need to be excused from physical activity on the days of Ramadan, in which they observe fasting from all food and drink. The academic calendar itself does not accommodate the Muslims who observe Eid, the largest and most important religious holiday of the Muslim calendar, in which they are not excused from school. With no accommodations, Muslim students fail to be welcomed into the "inclusive" public education system, being left alienated and without advocacy.

This feeling of alienation and insecurity within the public education system allows Muslim-American students to become vulnerable targets for bullying and hatred. The majority of Muslim-related education within the school curriculum is intertwined with terrorism education, which creates a correlation between Muslims and the dark events of America's past. Muslim girls face even further alienation when they choose to put on a hijab (usually done during middle school years), making them an identifiable target and outcast to their non-Muslim peers.

INTRODUCTION

The Muslim-American student struggle has not gone unnoticed in the Muslim community. This book aims to not only highlight issues, but to highlight and elevate the voices of Muslim students, in an effort to give them a platform to share their personal experiences combatting Islamophobia. In what follows this introduction is a unique and diverse collection of voices, perspectives, and research alike which seeks out the truth of studying in America as a religious minority.

Chapter 1:

Muslim-Targeted Bullying in the Education System

THE BULLYING OF MUSLIMS IN THE AMERICAN EDUCATION SYSTEM

By Asad Gilani

"I was on the school bus and this...random guy... he was like 'Go back to your country you f-ing Afghan'... I felt horrible. I felt really bad. I mean, I was only in 7th grade; what am I going to do? I felt that, I mean, how ignorant American society is, [and] at the same time, why do they have a wrong image of us? And I wish that... all Muslims, including me, could stand up because I think that then we can really show America that we're not a bad religion. We don't teach violence; we teach tolerance."

(Female Muslim Student, Seward & Khan, 2016)

"I was packing up my backpack today, and my friend came up to me. He said he would accept the invite to my birthday party, but his mom isn't allowing him to come because he thinks we're terrorists".

Author of Equal Opportunity, Asad Gilani, 2017

"A Muslim student recalled how a Social Studies teacher who was talking about the Middle East once said, "This is the region of peace haters." This greatly embarrassed the student, and he began fearing that his non-Muslim peers would have the same "peace-hating" impression of him."

(Sabry & Bruna, 2007)

Perhaps the worst thing about these personal accounts is that they are all but one in a million. Rather, these sentiments expressed amongst Muslim students are almost universal at this point. For too long, Muslim students have been the direct target of attacks simply because of their faith. What's supposed to be one of the most sacred pillars of life, faith, is instead looked at as the bane of students' existence. Muslim students are forced to navigate an awkward crossroads of being too Americanized for their faith but too Muslim to fit in at school. Essentially, these instances of Muslim bullying can be separated into two categories: Direct forms of bullying, like physical attacks, and indirect forms of bullying, like microaggressions. Together, these direct and indirect instances of bullying form a deadly duo that stifles Muslims in the education system. What is supposed to be a system in which students can grow to their maximum potential is instead the root of hatred and attack. Classmates who are supposed to be helpers in one's personal growth are instead the aggressors of violent and verbal forms of bullying. Worst, teachers supposed to be the developers of students' intellectual gain are, in certain cases, the perpetrators of problematic Islamophobic sentiment.

In trying to eliminate the bullying of Muslim students, it's essential to get to the true root of the issue. The first major stem of this bullying would be student-on-student hate. The bullying of Muslim students starts as little as elementary school, so where are these students gaining such intensely hateful opinions about Muslims? Children, being notoriously sponge-like, absorb the beliefs and opinions of the people around them. So, the true roots of this issue are the parents and peers of these students. Various surveys from different sources all share the common denominator of Muslim hate. In fact, about half (49%) of Americans think some U.S. Muslims are anti-American, and a quarter (24%) think American Muslims support extremism (Pew Research Center, 2016). Adding fuel to the fire, the media portrayal of Muslims in recent years has extensively furthered the gap between Muslims and non-Muslims. Media outlets have been quick to villainize Muslims and do the complete opposite for non-Muslims. Take these two examples, both from the New York Times:

Regarding a **Non-Muslim** perpetrator:
"Those who worked side by side with him saw an amiable and intensely shy student with a quick smile and a laconic air, whose quirky sense of humor surfaced goofy jokes...There was no question that he was intelligent." *(New York Times)*

Regarding a **Muslim** perpetrator:
"He was enraged....you could tell he wanted to do something to whoever had slighted him...It was like I was staring into the eyes of Ted Bundy...he was incensed by the sight of two men kissing." *(New York Times)*

Right off the bat, the stark difference between victimization and villainization is evident. Despite both being heinous acts of disgusting violence, the inhumane magnitude of horror is not captured in the account of the non-Muslim perpetrator. Readers of this media immediately gain a negative opinion of Muslims, and it is only a matter of time before this trickles down to children. These acts of bullying are typically not the fault of naive children, but it's evident that the sources from which they are obtaining this Islamophobic information need to be stopped.

Further, this bullying is not only limited to student-on-student attacks. In fact, there have been frequent accounts of teachers verbally and physically attacking Muslim children. Last year in South Brunswick,

New Jersey, a teacher faced criticism for using the movie, "Not Without my

Daughter," to teach her students about Islam (northjersey.com). Following the trend, the movie displayed Muslims as vicious terrorists and promoted negative ideas among students. This situation was most likely an indirect offense, as the teacher truly believed that Muslims were being correctly portrayed in the movie. Nonetheless, the negative portrayal hurt students in the classroom and ignited student-student bullying. The direct attacks on Muslim students among teachers are by far the most disturbing of all. In fact, in Maplewood, New Jersey, an elementary school student had her hijab ripped off by a teacher. According to the child's defense attorney, Cassandra Wyatt, "Ultimately, the teacher succeeds in pulling the hijab off her head, followed by a bizarre statement which is, 'Your hair is beautiful,'" the attorney said. "It is incredibly disturbing. It is very, very, symbolic of disregard of her religion and certainly something that has affected my clients overall." This ignorance of the importance and value of the hijab to Muslim women is one of many attempts to hurt Muslim students. Despite being the minority, teachers and their peers must ensure that Muslim students don't need to assimilate into the white American student archetype but, instead, are accepted for who they are.

Now that one can get a firmer grasp on the causes of the bullying of Muslim students, identifying its effects are just as important. According to FYI.org, "Discrimination and identity based bullying has been found to increase symptoms of depression and anxiety, as well as other internalizing (e.g. "I cry a lot") and externalizing (e.g. "I get in many fights") behaviors among

Muslim adolescents (Ahmed, Kia-Keating, & Tsai, 2011; Aroian, 2012; Dabbagh, Johnson, King, Blizard, 2012; Sirin & Fine, 2008). Hostility from peers and adults may contribute to Muslim adolescents internalizing anti-Muslim hate and questioning their self-worth (Sirin & Fine, 2008)." Students are silently suffering from issues that are fully out of their control. Muslims have no control over their religion, but they live in a society in which they are penalized for practicing it. The overwhelming majority of studies on mental health have all found a commonality which is that depression and bad mental health are direct causes of bad grades and academic activity. The true injustice at hand is the fact that Muslims are struggling in school, suffering from bad mental health, and enduring bullying, all for their faith. This puts Muslim students at a detriment; once again, the detriment is the effect of something they have no control over.

Moreover, another side of the mental health struggles that Muslim prejudice causes is an internal identity crisis. Muslim students often try to think one step ahead to avoid their religion putting them at a disadvantage to their peers. Muslim students have no choice but to assimilate into the pure American student archetype. This situation is prevalent in not telling people where they're from unless asked or making random excuses. From claiming they're going for a bathroom break instead of admitting they're going to pray or claiming to be on a diet to avoid the discussion of fasting, many Muslim kids are sadly quick to avoid any conversation relating to religion. Islam is a religion of love and community, and although it doesn't need to be worn on a badge by anyone, it certainly shouldn't be forcefully hidden due to other peoples' discriminatory acts. Muslim students slowly inch away from their faith, causing further internal struggle. Being a culture hybrid is almost looked down upon, and Muslim students are forced to choose between their Muslim faith or their American archetype. In eliminating this discrimination, Muslims' mental health will only be bettered, and the direct effects of negative mental health can also be fixed.

So, what can be done? The first step would be normalizing Islam as a religion. Although legislators and non-Muslim citizens have felt there is no need for halal foods in school cafeterias and prayer spaces, one can now identify a clear and concise reason for doing so. The argument against these various Muslim benefitting issues is that they only serve a minority of students, Muslims, so they are pointless. In reality, Islam is the second largest religion in the world, and the Muslim student population is only set to increase. Not to mention that no matter the population, all constituents of schools should and must be respected and accepted in their respective school environments. Past the acceptance edge of this, it's even more important to note that having these Muslim-benefitting reforms made in schools normalizes Muslims as regular peers and students, not as a monstrous, isolated group of individuals.

Promoting Muslim acceptance through small reform is only the first step; a firm and specific bullying policy is also needed to protect Muslim students in schools. Similar to the several bullying campaigns that have gained popularity in the recent decade, a similar approach is necessary for Muslim students' emotional, physical, and intellectual safety. As previously mentioned, in some extreme instances, teachers could be the root cause of bullying. Also previously mentioned, this comes from a point of ignorance. So, an easy solution would be for anti-bullying workshops and seminars to better identify bullying and prejudice towards Muslims. Further, these workshops can help teachers re-work curriculum to eliminate problematic sentiments regarding Muslims. From inferring Muslims are nothing but terrorists and violent people to ignoring the struggles they face. Acts of violence and terrorism on behalf of Muslims are a vital part of U.S. history and should not be justified. With that said, generalizing these terrorist attacks to the whole Islam-practicing population is dangerous and leads to all different routes of attack and hatred towards innocent Muslim students.

MUSLIM-TARGETED BULLYING IN THE EDUCATION SYSTEM

Beyond small-scale efforts amongst teachers, large-scale motions of legislation must be passed to ensure the safety of Muslim students in the classrooms. Islamophobia-backed bullying has progressed from schoolyard teasing to a brutal murder, so the lack of urgency among legislators to protect their Muslim constituents is beyond alarming. Federal law does not even touch upon bullying in the school system, let alone bullying towards Muslims. From the Civil Rights Act of 1964 still not being passed to the lack of other Muslim-protecting legislation, American policymakers must wake up. A great start would be amending certain acts that have already been written out, waiting to be picked up by the U.S. Government. A great example of this would be the "Safe Schools Act," which, if passed, "would prohibit bullying and harassment based on a student's religion, race, color, national origin, sex, disability, sexual orientation, or gender identity." (CAIR CA). However, the American federal legislative houses have stayed silent regarding the bullying issues at hand in schools, when there are drafted acts ready to help the cause instantly.

Due to the lack of efforts by the higher-ups of American law, the least one can suggest is small tweaks parents and peers can make to ease the stress and effects of bullying for Muslim students. For one, parents can stay vigilant regarding their kids and any sudden changes exhibited. Unfortunately, children often silently struggle and don't share their experiences of being bullied, as they feel weak. In fostering a healthy parent-child environment, children can be more open in telling their parents. If parents find out about acts of discrimination towards kids, they should not accept this as a part of growing up. It is the obligation of schools to act in situations of bullying, and there is a universal district policy that enforces this. So, it is essential to report any type of bullying to the school, to quickly rectify the issue at hand and simultaneously penalize the aggressor for their part in bullying Muslim children.

Moreover, parents should instill an iron fist in their kids and promote defending themselves. Muslim students often stay quiet and feel they are rightfully being bullied. They, too, need to be educated on who they are and stand for to avoid instances like these.

All in all, it is crystal clear that the rising rate of Muslim students in school should have no direct correlation to the rise of bullying towards Muslim students. It is essential for America as a whole to eliminate its pattern of the discrimination-acceptance pipeline. From the beginning of time, America has always forcefully assimilated and attacked different people before eventually accepting them into society. This has been the scene in African-Americans going from slaves to achieving the right to vote, and members of the LGBTQ+ community going from a stigmatized and hated community to earning the right to inter-sex marriage. Despite the reform that has taken place being commendable, not one American citizen should have ever gone through that discrimination. No American should be forced to undergo years of generational hatred before being accepted. Acceptance is not a trophy; it is a natural right. The opinions and false narratives spread across the media only fuel this raging fire. Opinions and news have never spread faster than now in modern-day America, so it is more than essential to ensure that any and every bit of news being published and circulated is entirely true, especially regarding Muslims.

Schools should be safe intellectual hubs where students can socially and intellectually grow safely, not a place of fear and hatred. The American population must be better informed about who Muslim people are and what they stand for. Further, America's legislative houses, from federal to local, need to step in and help their constituents in dire need of help. Without these proper protections in place, Muslims are put at a disadvantage in the education system. School is the stepping stone to the future of America, and it is the last place where the safety and growth of any child be compromised. The discrimination Muslims face in schools can lead to lifelong psychological effects on Muslims and stifle their growth for decades to come. So, it's clear that this is not a Muslim issue; It's an everyone issue. Americans must represent the pillars on which their country was founded and unite to help the silent sufferers of the school system, Muslim students. No child should be held back from their maximum potential, so putting the various political and social reforms in play is essential for the Muslim-American population's future. As a united force rallying for change, a better future of equal opportunity is guaranteed for the Muslim population.

INTERVIEW WITH ALAYNA KHAN, JUNIOR IN HIGH SCHOOL

Interview Conducted by Asad Gilani

Gilani: Hi Alayna! How are you?

Khan: Hi Asad! I'm great, and looking forward to sharing my experience.

Gilani: Absolutely! Why don't you go through a little bit of your experience as a Muslim in high school.

Khan: Yup! So being a minority in the school district, I always kinda ignored the religion/race questions. I slid by people assuming I was Latina and Christian, and since I didn't wear a hijab or anything, there was no visible sign labeling me Muslim. However, this all changed in 2016. 2016 was an awful year for Muslims. For starters, President Donald Trump was sworn into office, an absolute Islamophobe who proudly boasted about his "Muslim Ban". Furthermore, terrorism and mass shootings were through the roof at the time. The ultimate turning point for me was the Orlando nightclub shooting, in June 2016. There were whisperings of the attack being backed by homophobia, as it was a gay bar. I was horrified either way, and couldn't believe that someone would take such hatred to a physical level, killing almost 50 people. However, my terror was only elevated when the shooter's background was announced: He had pledged his allegiance to ISIS in advance of this attack. Just as a reminder, ISIS is a group of Muslim extremists that turn to terrorism to get their extremist beliefs across.

Gilani: Wow, absolutely horrific. And do you think there's anything worth noting as far as ISIS's connection with Muslims?

Khan: Yeah. Islam is a very peaceful religion, and the true meaning of Islam gets very misconstrued in the media. These violent acts of terrorism do not represent Islam's true principles and pillars. Unfortunately, people seem to not be able to separate these vicious disgusting terrorists from peaceful and normal Muslims like me.

Gilani: I think that's a great point you make, and this false assumption of Muslims is what often leads to bullying. From what you've told me previously, that's what happened in your case, correct?

Khan: Unfortunately, yeah. I was invited to a good friend's birthday party, and she approached me at my locker a few days after the shooting. Unbeknownst to me, they had found I was liking some pro-Muslim content on social media, and saw comments wishing me "Eid Mubarak" last year. They put the pieces together and realized I was Muslim, which kickstarted the confrontation. This girl approached my locker and told me, and I quote, "Hey Alayna! You actually can't come to my birthday because my mom doesn't want any terrorists there. She wants to limit the dangerous people in my life, and fears you and your family are some of them." Wow. Just wow. I honestly was questioning if it was real life. How could I be facing the implications of some random psycho? That's truly what I was asking myself.

Gilani: Right, and how did you look at your peers for support? For example, did you look to your school administrators?

Khan: To my shock, I really didn't have that support system at school. I don't know if it was targeted or not, but it was more so of the fact that teachers weren't really aware of what I was going through. I feel as though teachers don't have the proper knowledge or training to deal with situations involving racism or religious discrimination. As far as speaking to guidance counselors and my principal, I think they just gave a figurative slap on the wrist to some of the children, but nothing harsh enough for them to stop. Frankly, them not doing enough puts a huge strain on my mental health. I found myself having anxiety about going to school. Every time an act of terrorism occurred I knew it would bite me in the back when I came back to school. The feeling was torture, and it really messed with my self worth. I originally had such a strong inner identity of what it meant to be Muslim, even though I didn't shout it off the rooftops or anything. However, post all of this hate, I wanted to distance myself from the religion, in order to better my day to day life.

Gilani: And did you ever feel that these mental health and general self-worth issues had further implications on your grades as well?

Khan: Yeah. I basically lost all my friends and became that loner kid that sat by herself at an isolated lunch table. I felt I had no reason to live or to prosper, and started really slacking off. This left my grades lower than they ever were, because I really didn't have any passion to study.

Gilani: Wow. It is really so heartbreaking to hear that so many muslim students have such horrible experiences of bullying, but looking at you now you radiate confidence and happiness. Why the change?

Khan: I think for me, the biggest thing is knowing your personal worth and not letting anyone else affect it. I came to the realization at one point that the opinions that other racist people at school had on me had no impact on my day-to-day life. I realized what mattered most was who I was as a person and what that truly meant. I had this eye opening conversation with my mom, who wears a hijab. I would listen and the things people were saying to me at school, and she responded with, "So?

If someone calls you blind will you care? If someone calls you a giraffe, will you care? No. Because you know it's not true." This not only built me a thick skin but also helped me understand that it is not so much about what other people say, it is whether or not their words have weight to them, and their vicious words were not at all constructive. So, I learned to ignore the stereotypes and move on. And I have to say, I've never been happier.

INTERVIEW WITH HIGH SCHOOL BULLYING SPECIALIST, ANONYMOUS

Interview Conducted by Asad Gilani

Gilani: Hi! How are you?

Anonymous: I'm doing pretty good, and looking forward to getting started!

Gilani: Nice. Now I know you wanted to remain anonymous, but I think giving a brief background of yourself would be great for the readers to get a scope of you as a person.

Anonymous: Sure! I work as the Head High School Bullying Specialist at my high school and have headed this department for over 20 years. In leading this department, I take up all cases of bullied children whether this is reported by the bullied child, their parents, or their peers.

Gilani: Amazing, and I'd like to start off by commending the work you do with children, especially with mental health being such a relevant issue amongst children these days. To zoom in, have you ever dealt with an example of discrimination based bullying? If so, could you elaborate?

Anonymous: Well, I have dealt with quite a few of such cases. This is due to the fact that the minority population at the high school has tripled in recent years, and some of their counterparts haven't done so well with that. We've had black students called the n-word, we've had Jewish boys have their yarmulke ripped off, and we have had Muslim students called "terrorists".

Gilani: And what do you feel is the common denominator with all of these scenarios?

Anonymous: The common denominator is that the administration has limited us on how much or how little we can say regarding these forms of political correctness. Unfortunately, the conventional high school wants to stay out of all race relations, so much of the stuff we've proposed has failed. In order to better integrate our minority students into the high school, for example, we offered to start a bunch of different clubs, like a Muslim Students Association and an African American Heritage Club. The administration shut down every single one because of the mere fact that they had buzzwords in the titles that were harmful to the reputation of the school. Likewise, when dealing with these cases, we are stopped from sympathizing with these kids a lot because the administration makes it known that we can't do much in cases of discrimination.

Gilani: What can and can't you do?

Anonymous: Well, for example, we often had to shift the topic somewhere else. For instance, if one student called a Muslim student "Osama Bin Laden" then we would have to connect the two kids, and basically tell the bullied child that his bully was really mad over something else, and just took it out the wrong way. In fact, the bully probably did mean the hateful things he said, but we were just trained to swerve out of the conversation as fast as possible. It gets tricky because there needs to be a separation of church and state, and schools are state institutions. So, unless something is extremely hateful, we have to allow kids to have religious opinions that are still heavily hurtful

Gilani: Wow, super heartbreaking to hear. Now, what do you think can be done to make it better for these discriminated students?

Anonymous: I think the first step is an acknowledgment that there is a problem for minority students, we really have to stop gaslighting them into thinking whatever's happening to them is ok. Secondly, I think we should inform teachers and bullying specialists about some of the terminology and issues that certain students face, and then find a way to rectify the bullying. I think if we crack down on discrimination, just the overall school environment will be better.

Gilani: And what do you think the future implications of this discrimination are, if nothing gets done?

Anonymous: I think that the discriminated students would have much better lives, and truly believe they can accomplish so much more. No child wants to walk into the school being afraid of what someone will say to them, their main priority should be to learn. Students often don't recover from these signs of bullying and can grow up as under confident and low achieving adults, just because they truly believe they cannot do or accomplish anything anymore. Many say most of one's growth happens when they're an adult, but it's important to note that as a child the basic building blocks and pillars of that future growth are laid. Having a rocky foundation will screw over the entire building, so we need to demand change now.

THE DAY EVERYTHING CHANGED

A Short Story by Zara Gilani and Asad Gilani

Even though it has been weeks now, I can still remember September 11, 2001 like it was yesterday. Perhaps, I always will.

The day started off like any other. My mom woke me up at 6:30 in the morning. I listened to my shower radio, the one I got for my sixteenth birthday, a few weeks before. I spent way too long picking out an outfit. I ate breakfast, Cheerios and orange juice, in the kitchen while my dad did the crossword in the newspaper. My mom kissed my forehead goodbye before leaving for the hospital where she works as an obstetrician. My brother Omar, played on his Gameboy until dad told him he needed to hurry or else he would miss the school bus.

It was a sunny Tuesday morning and dad drove me to school early, so that I would have time to lock up my cello before my first class. That afternoon I was supposed to audition for the orchestra. I wanted to impress my music teacher with how much I had improved over the summer.

I dropped my cello off in the music room and ran into my best friend, Kate, in the hallway. She told me about her date with a boy named Xavier from the grade above the night before. They went out for ice cream and played mini-golf. I rolled my eyes when Kate told me that Xavier might be the love of her life.

We walked to our first-period classes. Kate had English and I had Calculus. At 8:15 a.m., the late bell rang. Moments later, the class stood

EQUAL OPPURTUNITY

and faced the small American flag hanging by the wall clock while the national anthem played through the loudspeaker. With our right hands over our hearts, twelve hundred students in fifty different classrooms recited the pledge of allegiance in unison.

The math lesson started and I tried to pay attention the best I could, but I was preoccupied with my orchestra audition coming up later in the day. Our teacher, Mr. Hanson, was assigning textbook problems for homework around a quarter after nine when we heard the loudspeaker go off again. Surprise announcements were rare. What would the principal say? A fire drill? Maybe an early dismissal? I don't think anybody would have guessed what he said.

"Good morning students and staff. Sorry for the interruption, but I have important news to share. I have just received a call informing me that two planes have crashed into the World Trade Center towers. We realize that this may be alarming to some of you. But as of right now, I want to let you know that we have no reason to believe you are not safe here at school. The class schedule will continue as normal. If teachers wish to turn on the news in their classrooms that will be allowed for the remainder of the day. Parents may be arriving early to pick up students. If that applies to you, we will make a phone call to your classroom and you will report to the main office to sign out. Thank you."

The abrupt message left us all shocked. My classmates started to murmur and exchange worried glances. I don't think Mr. Hanson knew exactly what to do. For the first time, I realized that teachers could be caught off guard too. After instructing us to finish jotting down the homework, he pushed the boxy television strapped to a cart out from the corner of the room. With a click of the remote, a fuzzy image of a news reporter appeared on the screen. I felt my body get heavy and my stomach drop. This wasn't just a plane crash, it was an attack.

The next few classes were a blur. I didn't talk much to anyone. Thankfully, each of my teachers allowed us to watch the news. I don't think I could have focused on anything else. By mid-morning, we found out a plane had crashed in a field in Pennsylvania. That's when I felt scared. Somerset county is not that far away from my hometown in the Lehigh Valley. Students were trickling out of classrooms to go home and be with their families. I almost cried in relief when the phone rang and my history teacher told me that my dad was here to take me home.

After signing out in the office with shaking hands, I nearly ran out to Dad's minivan in the parking lot. "Dad!" I sighed. He wrapped his arms around me in a warm hug and Omar soon joined in from the backseat. Instead of going home, we went over to my grandparent's house. Mom was already there. She had canceled her appointments for the rest of the day. She told us that in times like this you should have your loved ones near. Until midnight, the six of us prayed, watched the news, and prayed some more.

I felt so grateful that none of our family was in those planes or towers. I felt shared resolve and indignation when President Bush addressed the country. But when I laid down in bed alone that night, a new feeling took over me. Betrayal.

These terrorists used the name of my god to kill. How could they? Their beliefs were so different from mine, yet we all called ourselves Muslim. I was confused. I fell asleep with a headache and a wet pillowcase.

The next day at school is when I first started to notice a change in my classmates. If students were talking about the attacks, they would suddenly grow quiet and change the subject when I joined in with something to add. Whenever teachers would use words related to Islam a few stares would burn into the back of my head.

What hurt the most was when Kate started to act differently around me. It started gradually. She would call less and less and make excuses when I asked to hang out. Then, a few weeks later she told me she wanted to sit with some different friends at lunch for a change. I choked back tears and was told it was no big deal before ducking to eat in the bathroom. I knew it was all over when she told me that she couldn't go on the camping trip to Knoebels Amusement Park with my family we had been planning for months. "It's not you, Mahnoor," she tried to assure me over the phone, "It's my dad. You see he just is, you know, he thinks certain things and it's hard to change his mind. I told you about his cousin, the firefighter who passed. We just went to the funeral last week and… Listen, I'm sorry. Maybe next year, okay?"

In my typical fashion, I pretended that everything was just fine. "Okay, I get it," I said. I get that your Dad doesn't want you to hang out with me because I'm a Muslim and maybe you don't either, I thought. The worst part was I had no one to talk to about it. My parents were proud Muslims. If I told them, I thought that it would hurt their feelings and their pride. So I kept everything bottled in tight, leakproof in my heart except for midnights when my family was fast asleep and my body could shake silently with sobs.

I was happy the next day when I found that I had ranked first cello in the orchestra. My mood changed when at rehearsal the director asked me if it would be okay for someone else to play the "Silent Night" solo parts in the winter concert. He reluctantly explained that the audience might think it was more appropriate. He promised me a special part in the spring concert, but it did little to make me feel better.

This year was supposed to be my year and suddenly I felt like an alien in the town I had lived in for my entire life. At home, I became withdrawn. I spent most of my time praying for things to get better, and being disappointed when they never did.

The first week of October, a photography company came to the school to take our pictures for the yearbook. A dozen or so students in alphabetical order were sent down to the gym to wait in line and have a few headshots taken. In my group, the girls stood in front of the line eager to have the most time in front of the camera. The boys stood in the back so they could goof around. I stood in between them feeling invisible. I pretended to be gazing around at the basketball trophy case when I heard laughter behind me, followed by quiet, followed by a yank.

I gasped and spun around. One of the boys had ripped my headscarf off and thrown it on the ground. "Not in my yearbook," he said confidently. The boys laughed and jeered at each other. The girls exchanged looks and smirked quietly. "It is America, after all. If you want to wear that, go back to where you came from," a girl named Candace said, "But I guess she wouldn't be able to go to school then would she?" Candance added under her breath to her friend. I recognized Candace from my Spanish class last year. She hadn't struck me as a bully before. In fact, I thought she was nice which made her comments sting even more.

I picked up my headscarf and shoved it back on quickly the best I could before running to the nearest bathroom. I locked myself into the handicapped stall and slid down onto the floor. My face felt like it was burning and waves of nausea washed over me. I pulled my legs into my chest and rested my head on my knees. Inhale slowly, exhale slowly. Close your eyes and count to twenty. I calmed myself down and readjusted my hijab in the mirror. All I wanted to do was disappear, but that wasn't an option so quietly I went back to class without having my picture taken. There would be retakes the next day anyway.

The next morning, I stared at my reflection in the mirror and combed through my fine, brown hair one final time. I decided I would not wear my hijab to school. I just couldn't go on feeling like an outsider.

I wanted friends. I wanted people to feel safe around me. I just wanted to be normal after everything I had gone through. My little brother pounds at the door. The knots in my stomach tighten.

"Give me a second!" I called out. Omar stomped his feet as he ran downstairs to complain to our mother. I was happy with the way I looked without my headscarf, but I worried about what my parents would say when they saw me.

Mom and Dad always made it clear that what I wore was my choice. When I turned thirteen, I didn't feel pressured to begin wearing a headscarf out in public. I felt excited. I love Allah and I love my religion. Wearing a hijab is a practice that makes me feel more connected to Islam and my community. As a young teenage girl, it made me feel grown-up and beautiful to start wearing hijab like my mother and aunts.

In school and around my friends, I learned to explain why I dress modestly and what it means to me. In Allentown, Pennsylvania, there was a small community of Muslims, but most of my classmates were Christians or Jews. I came to understand the natural curiosity other kids had about my religion and I never minded answering questions. Up until the fall of 2001, I hadn't cared about being perceived as different. But then everything changed and I thought that I would have to change too.

I heard a soft knock at the bathroom door and it jolted me out of my thoughts. "Mahnoor, is everything alright?" my mother asked in her always gentle voice.

"Oh, yeah, everything is fine," I said in an overly-chipper voice. I pinched the palm of my hand and bit my lip. I cannot, I will not cry, I thought. I splashed water onto my face and bravely opened the door. I smiled at my mother as if that is what I looked like every day on my way out the door to school.

My mother looked at me, her eyes like moonlight, she was trying to see into me and understand without using words.

"I, uh, I'm going without the hijab today," I said nonchalantly. "If that's okay," I added. My mother nodded slowly and wrapped her arm around me in a big, warm hug. "Of course, it is okay, my sweet girl." She leaned back and rubbed the back of her hand against the side of my face. She admired me for a moment before tucking a piece of hair behind my ear. "We will never force you. It is always your choice, you know that."

At that moment, I realized that she knew. She's known all that time, because it has been just as hard for her as it has been for me. There is so much now that I wanted to tell her then, but I knew it would hurt too much to say out loud so I just whispered, "I love you."

I went to school and besides a few stares from classmates, I was surprised to discover that nothing changed. Even without my hijab, I felt like I stuck out like a sore thumb. I wondered if it would just take a little while before people warmed back up to me. I promised that in a few months nobody would even remember what I looked like with a headscarf and I would be able to pass as one of the white girls everyone wanted to be friends with. I got a yearbook photo retake without a glitch which made me feel happy, but not as happy as I thought it would. I still ate my lunch in the bathroom.

A few weeks later, I picked up a copy of my yearbook photo from the secretary's office. On the school bus home, I carefully unwrapped it from its envelope. The girl in the picture had my eyes, my skin, my hair, and my smile, but somehow I didn't feel like I was looking at a picture of myself. I felt like I was looking at someone else. And I guess I was. I realized that taking off my hijab was like trying to hide a part of myself. Islam is a part of who I am and it hurt to feel like I need to hide that. I shoved the photo into my backpack. I didn't want to look at it anymore.

When I got home, Omar cheered me up by asking me to play on his Nintendo 64. I sort of forgot about my troubles while we were playing for a while until the phone rang. I got up to answer it expecting it to be one of the parents calling from work, but instead, it was Kate. "Hey, Mahnoor," she said nervously.

"Oh, hey," I said.

"Well, I just wanted to say that I miss hanging out with you."

I smiled and my head started to feel floaty. "Yeah, me too, Kate."

"So my Dad said that you can come with us to Dorney Park on Saturday if you want." "Yeah, that sounds awesome. I would like that a lot."

"Cool! We can pick you up around nine if that works. Oh and Mahnoor, can I ask you a favor?"

"Sure, what is it?"

"Could you just maybe not wear your hijab? I mean, I know you haven't been recently and I just think that maybe my family would appreciate it and then you know we just don't have to worry about it drawing attention or anything."

My gut dropped. I had the decision to make. Finally, I might start fitting in again, but what was the cost? I looked over at Omar in the other room who was waving at me to return to the game and suddenly my decision was easy. I knew that if he ever asked, I would never be able to look him in the eye and tell him that I chose to fit in over my religious beliefs.

"Kate, I thought you understood that hijab is an important practice to me because of my religion. I know that things have changed since the attacks. People view us Muslims differently, but I'm still the same person and I'm tired of trying to change myself. We don't have to be friends if you don't want to be, but you don't get to say what I can or can't wear."

Silence hung in the air like the breeze after a thunderstorm. A few moments later, I heard a beep. Kate had hung up the phone. A few weeks before, I would have cried, but instead,, I felt overwhelmed with relief and joy. Finally, I felt free to start being myself again. I knew that I had a family that loved me and the choice to follow my religion was all mine.

FUTURE IMPLICATIONS

By Saira Gilani

Growing up in the 80s as a Muslim girl now seems like a scene out of a movie. When I talk about it with my kids, the shocked faces and absurd reactions I get remind me that my experience was one of injustice. What I used to think was the norm as a Muslim student going to public school in Queens, NY is now seen as racist, wrong, and outrageous. As a member of corporate America, working at one of the "Big 4" accounting firms that boasts diversity and inclusivity (as many firms in the U.S. now strive to do), I am often reminded that I was once the blueprint for discrimination in schools.

I was an "Undercover Muslim" for the first 18 years of my life. That was how we survived, back then. I grew up in a time where no one in the USA really knew who Muslims were. No one knew what Eid was, what it meant to observe Ramadan, what it meant to wear a headscarf. My immigrant parents from Pakistan were very clear: assimilate as much as possible, keep your head down, avoid eye contact, study hard and mind your own business. In truth, what was ingrained in us by our parents was fear. A fear of being recognized as an imposter, as someone who didn't belong. A fear of rocking the boat, or not fitting in if we discussed our religious beliefs too much. We were told to never say we "don't" eat pork. Rather, "I prefer turkey, please" when the lunch lady would serve us a ham and cheese sandwich. When there was none, we wouldn't eat.

EQUAL OPPURTUNITY

When I got to university, the same feelings of fear were instilled in me followed. There was no saying "I don't drink alcohol." Rather, I didn't "like the taste." Anything that could make me come across as different, as an intruder, imposter, or someone who didn't belong, couldn't be said. Any reminder of the fact that I was Muslim had to be erased from my brain. In creating such a persona for myself outside of my home, it started to feel real at times. The line between who I was and who I projected myself to be often blurred, private with perceived reality. Am I really Muslim?

When on-campus interviews began in senior year of University in 1998, all the big 4 accounting firms came. The instructions were very clear: boys need to wear navy blue suits and girls need to wear navy blue skirt suits. All of a sudden, I had no excuses. My religion didn't allow me to wear skirts or outfits where I show skin. What would I do? What would I say? I couldn't tell them no– I'd risk the chance of losing a spot in my dream career, or worse, lose the false, non-religious identity I had spent years working on.

As I sit in my office 23 years later, I remember vividly sitting in that interview room… in a navy blue skirt. I have never worn a short skirt since that. But that day, I went against my religion, in effort to stay concealed in my identity and to not stir up issues based on my religion. I compromised my religion for the acceptance of others. And it worked– I got the job. But at what cost?

Up until I started working, I had never said to anyone "I am a Muslim." I kept trying to assimilate as my parents told me to years before. To this day, I shy away from confrontation. "I don't associate myself with a religious organization" or "I'm not really that faithful." Funnily enough, even in this day and age, as diversity and equality have become buzzwords within society, I still find fear on my tongue when the subject comes up.

Though I am a confident Muslim today, the scared and shy sixth grade girl nervous on the lunch line still lives within me

STRENGTH IN NUMBERS

By Dean Aminyar

Although I couldn't put my finger on it, I was always treated differently for some reason. I didn't stand out in particular or anything. Growing up, being Muslim seemed like a disadvantage. Ever since I was young, I was very gifted at many sports. Soccer, basketball, tennis, the list goes on. Yet, in every sport, I was addressed in the same way every time. "No way you're Muslim"

"I didn't think you were Muslim cause you are good"

"If you are Muslim, shouldn't you be playing cricket?"

In the 3rd grade, when I was playing soccer with my brother and my cousin, a group of kids came up to us and asked if they could play. At the time, we were much smaller than them, so who were we to say no? We ended up playing, and we were winning. This made the other group of boys mad, and then it happened. The biggest one came up to me. His face filled with anger, and he labeled me a "sand n-word".

I didn't know what it meant, but it sounded like it had hurtful intent. This was the first of many times this hurtful name-calling happened in my life, and it always seemed to come down to race or religion. As I grew up, I, unfortunately, noticed more and more of the gap between Muslim students like me and others.

In the 5th grade, I started fasting during the month of Ramadan. It was tough, but I still persevered through it. One day, I had a game while fasting, and I couldn't eat food or drink water, but I still went. I informed my coach about it so I could break my fast in the middle of the game. As soon as I told him, I could tell his thoughts had shifted. After that, when the game started, I sat on the bench the entire time. His excuse for not putting me in was that he didn't want me to be at a disadvantage because I couldn't drink or eat. My blood was boiling. I tried to explain to him that it didn't matter and I could play through but who is going to listen to a young kid?

This wasn't the first time my fasting was a problem. When I was in the 7th grade, fasting became a normal thing for me. One day, I was much more tired than usual and had gym last period. I told my gym teacher that I wouldn't want to partake in anything too energy-consuming, and she understood completely, but one day, we had a sub, and she forced me to run in the heat. She didn't care that I was fasting; if anything, she made it more challenging. I was struggling to breathe and felt nauseous, so I called my mom to pick me up from school. This changed my perception of how some teachers are. Some want what's best for you, and some will go out of their way to make you feel bad.

It got even worse from there.

I take pride in being Muslim, but sometimes it is hard to do at school.

The school was one of the worst experiences for me at times. Although I had my fun moments, I had a lot of bad experiences along the way. Every week, I would hear a kid yell "Allah Akbar" in the hallways and throw their bag as a "joke". But it is not. I just watched and felt helpless. I couldn't tell them to stop because I would start being made fun of, and they would just continue. Telling the principal wouldn't even help, either. The worst part was the teachers tolerated it. They didn't talk when the kids said racist things. They just minded their business, not caring. It was the worst on 9/11.

9/11 is a touchy subject for most, and it should be. Some Muslim extremists flew two planes into the World Trade Center, and now people have this terrible perception of Muslims around the world. There is no doubt that those people were disgusting excuses for Muslims. However, I was piled into their category. It hurt to think that after one bad moment, people stereotyped and judged every Muslim. On the memorial of the day, we were learning what happened. When the words were first said by my history teacher, everyone looked at me. Forty eyes just glaring at me. Some smirk and people whisper to each other. They acted like I did something. I wanted to give them a good idea of what Muslim people truly were, but I couldn't. At lunch, it got worse. Racist comments continued to be said. People were making jokes about Osama Bin Laden and the airplanes.

At that moment, I just wanted to leave school.

Being Muslim in a predominantly white school was challenging. Most kids were so entitled and just scummy. Not only was it the kids but even the school itself. Especially the lunch committee. I had to have the same thing every day. Pizza and chips. For a whole year. I knew they didn't have pork in them. My school didn't offer me these options to choose from as all the other kids did.

It extends further, too. I couldn't miss class for prayer times. It isn't fair that I can't practice my religion without being penalized for it. The school had no exceptions and didn't even provide any spaces or materials for me to pray. As a Muslim, praying is an important thing that many Muslims do. Not being able to pray is absurd for a school to do to a kid. I knew in my head things needed to be done. Muslim students and Muslim people around the world are treated differently and aren't given the same respect others are given.

This led me to want to make a change in how society perceives and treats Muslims. People have this idea that Muslims are so bad and evil, and the Quran is spreading very bad thoughts to its followers, and it is simply not true. This leads people to become Islamophobic which is as much a problem as it is sad. One voice isn't strong enough to combat the stereotypes that have been assigned to us, but together as a Muslim community, we can make a change. That is exactly what The Muslim Students For Justice are doing. They are letting people know the unfair treatment Muslim people get in the hope of swaying their thoughts on people.

I truly believe that we can make a difference together, but it isn't a one-person job. Muslims aren't the only ones being oppressed; many different people of different religions and backgrounds are treated badly. It is our job to come together and put a stop to it. Strength in numbers.

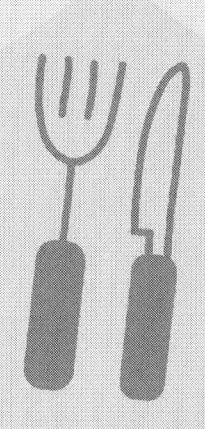

Chapter 2:

The Lack of Halal Options in School Cafaterias

THE LACK OF HALAL OPTIONS IN SCHOOL CAFETERIAS

Asad Gilani

Water.
Air.
Shelter.
Food.

Simple enough, right? No. Within the American education system, all but one of these natural needs are met. Students are supplied water through water fountains, shelter through roofs and supporting walls, and air. However, one basic need for human survival is not met, for millions at least. Millions of students go hungry at lunch every single day. While students with no restrictions eat freely from the school cafeterias, Muslims are left to choose between the two most sacred things: a basic human right or violating their religion. Despite years of complaints, legislators and educational officials have ignored Muslim's requests and pleas for halal options in school cafeterias. Officials have given Muslims improper and inadequate resolutions, such as packing their own lunch or eating vegetarian options. This isn't a matter of small-scale solutions; it's a matter of equality. No student should be denied the privilege of buying food when their peers can freely select their meals. Further, no student should be restricted to vegetarian options that consist of muffins, chips, fruits, and other nutritionally inadequate options. Historically,

Muslims have faced the challenge of being ignored by the government or the school system. Not to mention the domino effect of these issues and how Muslim students' test scores and grades suffer because of their hunger. For the sake of our future, it's time to break the chain and rally for an immediate solution to an urgent issue. This can guarantee a better future for Muslims around the country by rectifying this nationwide issue.

At most high schools in America, lunchtime overlaps with school hours. This has never proven to be an immense issue, as most high schools offer lunch options through their cafeteria. However, a distinct minority had been silently suffering. Halal eaters have been forced to bring their food or go hungry during school days. Further, it's been seen as presumptuous to even protest for cafeterias to offer halal options. Legislators have fought against halal foods, claiming that the higher prices would put school districts at a monetary disadvantage. Essentially, that's the core of the issue.

Legislators and school officials choose to ignore cries for proper food options valuing their pockets more than their students' basic human rights. The issue at hand is that a line needs to be drawn somewhere. Yes, it would be cheaper if there were no halal foods at school. Further, it would be even cheaper if schools didn't feed their students at all.

The goal is to find a healthy medium where everyone has nutritious and dietarily proper meals. These meals do not have to be halal filet-mignon or Chilean sea bass; they just need to be the basic school lunches already offered, with altered meats instead. Not only is this argument legit from a logical and moral standpoint but the logistics back it up.

In "Let Them Eat Lunch: The Impact of Universal Free Meals on Student Performance" by Amy Ellen Schwartz & Michah W. Rothbart, it was reported that "Results indicate that increases in school lunch participation improve academic performance for both poor and nonpoor students; an additional lunch every two weeks increases test scores by roughly 0.08 standard deviations in math and 0.07 standard deviations in ELA." (Amy Ellen Schwartz & Michah W. Rothbar). Schwartz and Rothbart discussed the disadvantage of not eating lunch for underprivileged students, but the same applies to halal eaters. Others have claimed that halal eaters have other options to satisfy their needs. The foods in question include chips, cookies, and sugary drinks. These weak alternatives give students a fraction of the necessary nutrients, like protein, needed to flourish in school. Further, officials scavenge for inadequate alternatives as their explanations promote an essence of religious tolerance instead of religious acceptance.

For most people, faith and education are two of the key pillars of life. The injustice the American education system brings to the table is that students are forced to choose between their faith and education. Going hungry throughout the school day presents an academic deficit to students. On the other hand, students can eat the food given but then have to deal with the guilt of breaking one of the most important laws in their religion, testing a part of their faith that would have otherwise gone untested. Something as simple as a carton of milk with chicken fingers to some is an immense struggle to others. No students should have to face the guilt of not abiding by their religion, nor do they have to face the consequences of starving throughout the school day.

Another popular counterargument is that students should just bring their food to school. It isn't even about that they could bring food from home; it is that they are denied an opportunity that non-Muslim counterparts are given. However, if the counterargument is broken down further, one could see that government-subsidized lunches are much cheaper than home-packed lunches, now putting a detriment on Muslim's wallets, in addition to their education and faith. Take the Keep Kids Fed Act, enacted into law in 2021. The Keep Kids Fed Act made all school lunches free for that school year. This was a great way to ease students back into school from the pandemic, especially considering the financial turmoil many families went through. Muslim kids were denied the right to enjoy this great opportunity, as the meals most schools were serving were not halal. This is just one example of many in which Muslim kids are disadvantaged from opportunities solely because they can't conform to the meal plan that schools are offering.

As mentioned before, most of the efforts to reform the cafeteria system have been either ignored or labeled presumptuous. Legislators from the federal level to the city level have felt that it is too much to ask to serve halal foods in school cafeterias, as they serve a "plethora" of other options. Halal food proposals have been rejected due to the fiscal damage they will do or because there are not enough Muslim students. To reiterate, money is nothing in the grand scheme of children going hungry in the classroom. So, it is clear that there is urgent reform needed, and religiously inclusive foods required in school cafeterias should be mandated into federal law.

Despite most school districts making weak excuses for offering halal lunches, some districts have successfully done so.

All in all, it's evident that no halal foods being served in school cafeterias is nothing short but an injustice. The domino effect of students going hungry and performing below average on tests is just as problematic as kids eating halal foods, denouncing their faith against their own wishes. No student should ever be faced with choosing between their faith and education; the only instant fix to this is federal reform. In mandating halal foods in cafeterias worldwide, the American Muslim population of 3.45 million Muslims will be properly fed and represented. It is crucial to ensure that all students do not face Muslim injustices at such a young age, shaping a future of racism and injustice for them. The multifaceted youth of the future need to be nurtured today, and providing an essential human right to them is instrumental to that nurturing.

AN INTERVIEW WITH NEW YORK CITY 37TH DISTRICT FORMER COUNCILMAN RAFAEL ESPINAL.

By Asad Gilani

Rafael Espinal was instrumental in introducing a halal foods pilot program to several of the schools he served. *Transcribed from "Contemporary Conversations," A Podcast by the Muslim Students for Justice Organization*

Gilani: Councilman Espinal! How are you?

Espinal: Hi, Asad; I'm doing great.

Gilani: Super excited to have this conversation today. For the sake of our readers, why don't you give yourself a brief introduction.

Espinal: For sure. All my life, I was always concerned about all the issues affecting my community. I grew up in East New York Brooklyn, a neighborhood with several socio-economic uses. With that, I always wondered why the city didn't invest in communities like mine as they did in other parts of New York (more affluent communities). After college, I took a job working for a local city council member and was instantly inspired to run. I saw an opportunity to resolve the issues that the city did not resolve in my community.

Gilani: That alone is pretty amazing. I think this is a great pipeline that should be a real archetype for the future. I think the best lawmakers and officials are people that have experienced the issues that they are fighting for. Following this train of thought, what ignited your cause to propose a Halal Foods Program for schools, being not Muslim yourself?

Espinal: Yeah. I guess I'll say one thing; I guess what resonates with me the most is when I learned about communities that are being underrepresented in the legislative process. Being that I grew up in a neighborhood that was underrepresented, I strive to fight for others. In the area where I live, there is a small community called the city line. In the city line, there is a growing Bengali Muslim population. One issue that became prevalent was that their children were going to school and would not eat lunch, as the schools don't offer halal options. Further, they didn't even offer a nutritious vegan option. Once this became known to me, I believed that the Department of Education should make sure that all children are being fed nutritious options, no matter the religious background.

Gilani: Right. Being a Muslim student myself, I feel that it's important to note the domino effect that this leads to. When children are hungry, they are not focusing on the source material in classrooms, as their minds rather train off into how hungry they are. So, I wanted to know if you specifically had to work with the Board of Education school by school or did you go straight to the Department of Education?

Espinal: It's a multilayered process. But before I get into that, I want to address the point you made. I think it's absolutely correct that Muslim students do worse in the classroom as a direct result of not having food. Officials often go to the curriculum when test scores are low, and students are doing worse when, in reality, key points like food are also real necessities. Back to your question, we initially spoke to the local school and learned from the principal that while the school had discretion on what was being served in their school because they ordered the lunches from the Board of Education, the Board of Education did not have a large budget, so they couldn't get halal foods. So, what the principal was able to do was find more vegan options, But unfortunately, vegan options meant a cold lunch, like a peanut butter and jelly sandwich. While this helped ease concerns in the immediate, we knew it wasn't a long-term fix. So, we needed to have a more solid fix. So, we started working with the agency in the state to ensure halal and nutritious options.

Gilani: Yeah. And once you proposed this halal foods program, did you face any significant pushback?

Espinal: Absolutely, one, of course, I think it's the question of bigotry. Folks have this very strong notion that you should not be mixing religion with our schools, but I think it has deep roots in racism and discrimination towards Muslims. Two, I think on a more technical aspect, it had to do with the cost of sourcing halal meats. I believe the costs of those meats were about four times higher than what the education system was accustomed to. So, it was important for myself and my colleagues to allocate funds directly towards the pilot program, which turned into millions of dollars.

Gilani: And do you think the racism was them wanting a separation of church and state?

Espinal: Yes, I think it really came from the taxpayer more than the department of education, and they didn't want to see their tax dollars spent on a program that doesn't fit their personal values.

Gilani: Yeah, I think it's important to note that when we try to propose this into our school system, we'll face similar pushback. So, when we propose this to our Board of education, how do you think we would refute the Board's potential issues with the halal foods program?

Espinal: I think it's just the data that shows the correlation between healthy school meals and student performance and the long-term impacts that would have on society; I think it's also key to make the correlation between the existing programs that exist in other cities and how successful they've been, just like mine. This has been seen across the country, from Dearborn, Michigan, to my district, to California. I think these serve as case studies to show how these could work anywhere in the country.

Gilani: Right. And just out of interest, did you have other projects that combated similar causes?

Espinal: Honestly, this was a big one for me. I focus a lot of time on focusing on food injustice from many different races. From people needing fresh food and vegetables to delis, there were a lot of environmental injustices with underrepresented communities that were often minorities. Especially health-related injustices, like asthma and diabetes. So these also connect back to foods, so this was really my main focus.

Gilani: Wow, that is truly amazing. I think zoning in on a specific niche is so important and even leads to what we're doing. Furthermore, I think it's interesting to know how everything is interrelated. With your specific interest in food injustice, did you ever wanna federalize your pilot program?

Espinal: Yeah, at the end of the day, the only way this pilot program could work is if it was federalized. The federal government is how this would be sustainable, as this is where most school lunch dollars come from. So, if we have enough cities and states implement pilot or permanent halal programs, we can definitely make the case that there needs to be more federal funding targeted toward feeding our students meals that they are able to eat.

Gilani: Absolutely. So, as we mentioned before, a key reason schools don't wanna enact halal food programs into their schools is because of the price, so how do you think the federal government would ease the hit?

Espinal: It's the subsidies. It comes down to the federal government giving the extra money that the school districts don't have. At the end of the day, looking past any racism, the cost is the main reason the districts point to the barrier. So, it's important that all advocated and allied groups talk to their federal leaders so when it comes time to vote on the next federal budget, there are these subsidies that exist to supply these halal foods.

Gilani: That's awesome, and this also leads me to the question of how long the process would take, especially since you needed to garner funding.

Espinal: It was an extremely long process. I was elected into the city council in January 2014, and it was only in 2019 that we finally were successful in the pilot program. This requires a lot of community involvement and a lot of advocacy. I would say this, what really helped us get to the finish line was when allied groups came together and became part of the process. This is why I think it's so important to build on advocacy groups and allies and make them aware of how it's important to be a part of these conversations.

Gilani: Great. With that, I thank you so much for your time today in discussing the maxing change you are giving to our Muslim community.

EQUAL OPPURTUNITY

I think it's especially amazing to see a non-Muslim be such a strong ally to our community and use your resources to help us.

Espinal: Thank you, I appreciate that. I'd like to leave off with my favorite quote, "An injustice anywhere is an injustice everywhere." I think this applies to this amazingly and shows how these efforts are allied efforts, not one-man jobs.

—

In having this conversation with Councilman Rafael Espinal, we can see how a change in our communities is hard but possible. This conversation should serve as a reminder that change is possible. Although one might feel small in the grand scheme of government, working together as allies is key to implementing change and reforming the injuries of Muslims around the country. In doing so, we guarantee a brighter future for Muslim students.

RICE KRISPIE TREAT, PLEASE!

A Personal Account by Asad Gilani

The loud chatter of "Pokemon Go" and "Avengers", apple sauce, and rice kernels spilled around the perimeter of kids' plates and long snack lines. Yup, that pretty much sums up the fifth-grade cafeteria.

Fifth grade was the first time any of us had a real cafeteria, and it was nothing short of a magical land, especially the snack line. My favorite snack to purchase at the snack line? Easy. Rice Krispie treats.

I know, quite the paradox for a Muslim. Of our religion's many dietary restrictions, we are forbidden from having anything pig-related. To give a quick rundown, Rice Krispie treats have marshmallows, marshmallows have gelatin, and gelatin is made of pig fat. So, there you go. Before the haram police, haram being anything Muslims cannot eat due to religious restrictions, handcuff me, let me explain.

It was October, one month into my cafeteria adventures. Like clockwork, I hit the snack line every day.

Side note: There were no halal options on the main line, which was quite an inconvenience. The spaghetti and meatballs, the sandwiches had turkey, and the hamburgers had beef. Halal meats need to be cut a certain way, and none of the meats offered at the school passed that test. So naturally, I could only stick to the snacks. And yes, I was by no means having a very nutritious lunch. But what could I do? It would cost more money for my parents to pack me lunch, as school lunches are

EQUAL OPPURTUNITY

government subsidized, so I wasn't gonna take an overly expensive lunch to school every day.

Anyways, back to my story. I had just won a bet with my best friend, so he was buying me a snack today. After waiting in line, we got up to the front.

"Hi, kids! What would you two boys like today?"

"I'll have the Rice Krispie treat. My friend's gonna have the same."

To be clear, I knew the Rice Krispie treat had marshmallows in it. But what was I supposed to do? I would never proclaim that I practice Islam just to save myself from that embarrassment. So, I ate the Rice Krispie treat. It tasted like delicious, sweet, crunchy *guilt*.

What had I just done? What a loser was I? Disobeying my faith after following it for ten years just to save myself from an awkward conversation?

I went home that day and prayed. I pulled a dusty extra prayer mat out of the hallway linen closet, laid it down, and prayed. I prayed for forgiveness; I prayed that Allah, God, would forget that I ever did such a thing.

The prayer clearly meant nothing to me because I continued this haram trend for months to come. Like clockwork, my best friend would arrive at the lunch table with an extra Rice Krispie treat for me. Better yet, I would slide him over a dollar to compensate him.

Wow, an all-time low. I was paying for haram food. But really, what was I supposed to do? Rice Krispie treats were the only snacks offered at the snack line, besides chocolate-covered marshmallows, which I felt were more haram on the haram scale anyway. So, I was really confused. Already as it is, my friends were chowing down on nutritious meals filled with protein and energy, and I was stuck eating my lousy little snack.

Besides my guilt, eating just little snacks had detrimental effects outside of the cafeteria. I was still left feeling hungry and more focused on what I would eat at home than on simplifying fractions. I felt the contingency sequence occurring. Having un-nutritious food led me to do worse in the classroom. Furthermore, it being haram only took a toll on my mental health, furthering a weakness in the classroom. Why was no one doing anything about this?

The same reason no one ever felt the need to help us Muslims; we were a minority. Despite learning about the American heroes that fought against racism and achieved the right to vote for women, this activist energy was anything but consistent. The Muslim population at my middle school was only on the uprise, but our accommodations were stagnant.

I knew a change needed to be made. Lacking the knowledge of professionalism and the formalities of talking to higher-ups, I marched right up to my principal. He was on lunch duty, so he surely had time to speak with me. I firmly explained my practiced string of dialogue, hoping I would get some form of sympathy and he would set a slew of reforms into place. However, I just got a measly reply:

"No worries, Asad. We're opening a salad bar soon!"

Great, more mediocre food. With no meat, of course, I would be graduating from snacks to cucumber and arugula married together by bottled Italian dressing! I mean, these school administrators were supposed to be the ones that looked out for us; instead, they gave this! I just wanted the battle to end. No, not a physical one. The mental one.

The sad reality was that even my weak attempts at reform were too overwhelming for me. Being completely ignored and unheard was enough to turn me off from fighting for change. It seemed to be true; minorities like us were constructed to suffer silently.

So, what did I do? Nothing. I continued eating Rice Krispie treats and would get really crazy on the days I had the turkey sandwiches. Could you blame me? Seven hours with no food?

Inhumane! Honestly, it wasn't that bad. So many pillars of Islam, and all I was breaking was a fraction of one? Sounds like a plan. At the end of the day, my basic human needs trumped any faith. I led my life with this ideology for a while before yet another mental breakthrough.

Who was I? What was I doing? I was spiraling into this force of self-destruction, disobeying the religion I once followed with utmost faith.

It felt like that falling feeling just when you're about to go to bed. Dozing off, Dozing off, then BOOM! You snap out of that falling feeling and wake up with a heart rate spike. Falling into this haram black hole was my dozing off fall, and this sudden awakening was the BOOM!

I then realized that the only thing worse than eating haram foods was gaslighting myself to believe that that was ok. I mean, really, who had I become? But the thing was that it wasn't even my fault. I couldn't function on an empty stomach. My grades would slack, and I wouldn't be able to think straight. There were two sides to the tug of war: the administration and me. They could change and offer more halal food. Or I could break my faith. I had already done that, and all of the guilt and shame that followed proved to me it was an unworthy cause. So, it was the final straw

I rallied all of the Muslims together, as much as I knew. And then, we scheduled a meeting with the administration.

Fast forward a year later...

Within one year, I rallied with my fellow Muslims, secured funding, and initiated a halal foods program at school. Yeah, yeah, we got all of the halal meat at school for nutritional purposes. But I made sure we also secured a box of halal rice crispy treats. Never again did I have to worry about the guilt I would feel upon ordering at the snack line. Funnily enough, my order never changed.

"Hi! Rice Krispie treat, please!"

Chapter 3:
The Detriment of Eid Not Being Acknowledged as a School Holiday

THE DETRIMENT OF EID NOT BEING ACKNOWLEDGED AS A SCHOOL HOLIDAY

By Mehreen Khateeb

Atlas, the ultimate test of your faith is done. After a month of strenuous days of fasting, the celebration of Ramadan's end has begun. Eid, a celebration often referred to as "The Muslim's Christmas," is a time of joy, happiness, and quality time with friends and family. Despite its importance to Islam and Islam's constituents, countless schools don't acknowledge it as a religious holiday in their calendars, leaving many students at a disadvantage upon their return and throughout the year.

Eid is celebrated twice a year, one being Eid al-Fitr and the other, Eid al-Adha. Eid al Fitr, in countries like Afghanistan and Pakistan, is "a three-day celebration in Muslim-majority countries. But in the United States, it's generally observed on one day" (USA Today). Naturally, it makes sense for the American Muslim population to adapt to American culture, even if it means cutting celebrations short because, in America, the norm for holidays is a single day, with the return to school and work the following day. Now, when referring to the holy holiday, many will reference a one-day holiday, disregarding its roots from a three-day holiday.

All over the country, one can easily notice the plethora of school holidays given for religious holidays, from Christmas to Rosh Hashanah.

EQUAL OPPURTUNITY

Despite varying schedules, the common denominator of schools around the country is the complete ignorance of Eid. In 2017, there were around 3.45 million Muslims in the United States, a rate that is only projected to increase (Pew Research Center).

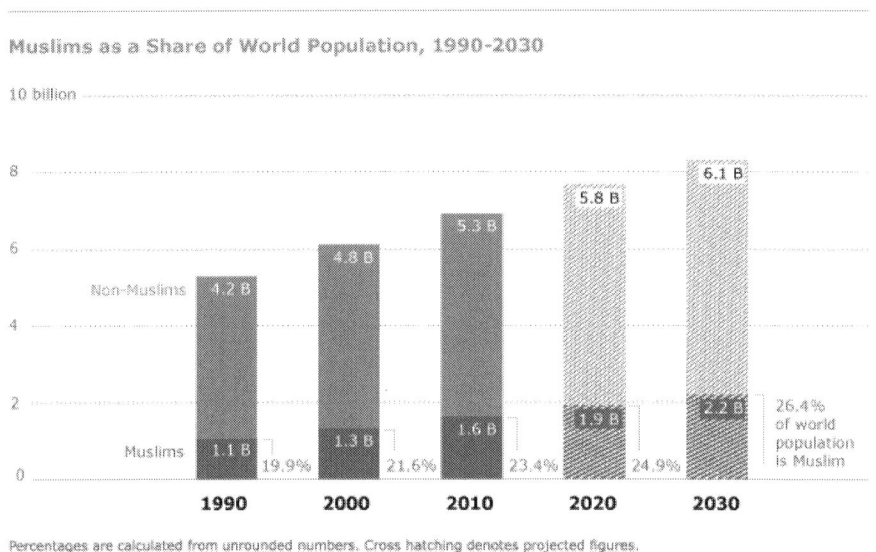

Muslims as a Share of World Population, 1990-2030

Year	Non-Muslims	Muslims	% Muslim
1990	4.2 B	1.1 B	19.9%
2000	4.8 B	1.3 B	21.6%
2010	5.3 B	1.6 B	23.4%
2020	5.8 B	1.9 B	24.9%
2030	6.1 B	2.2 B	26.4%

Percentages are calculated from unrounded numbers. Cross hatching denotes projected figures.

Pew Research Center's Forum on Religion & Public Life • *The Future of the Global Muslim Population*, January 2011

(Rising numbers of Muslim population into future, Pew Research Center)

However, schools have made the universal claim that the Eid attendance is not substantial enough to close schools. Looking closer at the University of Delaware's attendance policies, they advocate for encouraging "not to schedule examinations or require the submission of special assignments on Eid al-Fitr." This weak justification leaves students feeling not only unseen, but getting marked down absent, despite valid reason. Schools may make the effort, like the University of Delaware, to seem inclusive and representative, but it isn't enough. Students now have to choose between faith and school, but that shouldn't ever be the case. Students should be able to freely focus on their faith and do their best in school at the same time. Giving Eid a day off for everyone means that the students who do celebrate don't have to worry about coming back to school the next day with twice the amount of homework, the confusion of the missed lessons, and the tests and quizzes they need to make up. Let a kid celebrate and worship in peace. The evidence the Muslim community has on this concept is clear, there isn't a day off for Eid and that results in Muslim students feeling a lack of inclusivity and belonging. Neva Khan, a junior at Lake Ridge High School claims "...It's a courtesy. I remember when I was little and missed school for Eid I had to get a note from the mosque. It's like, why do I have to justify myself with a religious excuse? I think it's super unfair. Muslims and our holidays just get overlooked in the grand scheme of things," (Eagle Nation News). When students are going out of their way to say this, it raises the question of why there are still schools out there that feel that the policies they currently have are permissible. To defend their stance, schools rush in "...explaining that the number of observant students was not large enough to necessitate shutting down schools" (northjersey.com). Not only does this belittle the Muslim community, but it's generally inconsiderate. Claiming that with Muslim students absent on the day of, there is no difference, gives just another reason for students to feel invalid, and pushes the movement to have Eid a national holiday, in general. Starting off with one district will easily create a ripple effect, meaning when one district implements the policy of having Eid marked as a day off due to a national holiday, other districts will follow, realizing the way such practices before were portraying injustice towards Muslims. With schools making claims that their absence made no difference, it'll prevent such steps forward.

EQUAL OPPURTUNITY

(Thousands in prayer for Eid al-Adha at MetLife Stadium, northjersey.com)

In order for future generations to be able to experience such a holiday with ease, it's time Eid should be recognized as a national holiday. All the Muslim community asks for is one day off in the three-day celebration for their kids to fully embrace their religion, and this is how to get it. Beginning by starting off small always makes a difference, whether it's gathering the community to attend district board meetings, sending emails to the people in control of the district's school system, or reaching out to local news broadcasts to voice your concern. Even on a small scale, it's essential for Muslims and Muslim allies alike to rally to lawmakers and local education officials for acknowledgment as a religion worthy of a holiday group of people. Signing petitions on government websites like "We The People" is just one way Similarly to "We The People," there are other websites, such as Change.org, that offer multiple petitions revolving around Eid getting noticed in areas all over the world. The more people that sign the petitions, whether its fellow Muslims or helpful members of the community that want to assist in the fight against such injustice, the more recognition amongst authorities like Congress, or any sort of government authority to look into the issues at hand for the Muslim community. All of these methods require patience, but that doesn't mean waiting around after trying once is an option. Starting now and constantly advocating for Eid being a day off in a district is one step closer to Eid being acknowledged amongst all schools. Eid being acknowledged amongst all schools will easily have students feel accepted and know that their attendance and presence in school matters.

(One of the multiple petitions for Eid to be recognized as a holiday, Change.org)

To summarize, now is the time to urgently reform the American school system to put a full stop to Islamic injustice. The first step would be indirect injustice, such as not getting Eid off. Not counting Eid as a holiday is not a deliberate discriminatory act by any means, but it promotes a sense of ignorance whilst promoting a lack of tolerance. That shouldn't be the case, and students should feel accepted in the sense that the school should be giving a day off for Eid because they understand the importance of the religious holiday. Not only will the administration recognize Eid, but students who aren't Muslim and will be staying home for the holiday will know why they are home and generally, know that the holiday exists. Those students at home will put themselves in a position to be well aware of the Islamic holiday taking place that day, similar to the Muslim kids at home on Christmas, knowing what Christian students are doing in their homes, whether it's praying, opening gifts, embracing the warmth that surrounds them, and more. Though it seems small and indifferent compared to other "solutions" in combating Muslim injustice, it will serve its purpose when Muslim families all over the world can naturally accept that it's Eid, a time when families are meant to be home, or in areas of prayer, instead of in school. Always remember that there are many people, communities, and cities, fighting for the same fight, and in the end, in hopes of a better future for the Muslim community, change needs to start now and grow otherwise Eid won't receive the recognition a holy holiday deserves, and it's necessary in order to create a better future for oncoming generations.

INTERVIEW WITH KHAJA KHATEEB, PRESIDENT OF THE NJ EID COMMITTEE

Interview conducted by Mehreen Khateeb

M. Khateeb: Hello Khaja, thank you so much for meeting with me today and discussing the injustices Muslim students face not having Eid recognized as a school holiday. So first, I think it would be great for you to give a small introduction of yourself.

K. Khateeb: My name is Khaja Khateeb and I'm a professional pharmacist and a businessman. I have a pharmacy in New York City where I have worked for the last thirty years, and I have another pharmacy in Hackensack, New Jersey. Just some background, I migrated from India and I've been living in Paramus, New Jersey for 22 years.

M. Khateeb: Alright, thank you for that introduction! I'm also going to go ahead here and give a small introduction to the readers as to who I am and what I'm doing here. My name is Mehreen and I sit on the executive board here for the Muslim Students for Justice, and I'm here to talk a little more particularly on the injustice that we face on Eid, more specifically attendance policy

and how that correlates to Eid not being recognized as a national holiday. I've wanted to talk about this for a while with you because you're the President of the Eid Committee. So I'm going to go ahead and start off with some introductory questions so the listeners have some background information before we do talk about the main issue at hand, so if you can, please go into what the Eid Committee actually is.

K. Khateeb: The Eid Committee was formed in 2004 just to make sure the Eid prayer arrangements for the Muslim community in Bergen County, well, not only Bergen County, but in all of New Jersey, were set in stone. So the Eid Committee began making arrangements in 2004 at Teaneck armory and we brought together all these mosques that would usually pray individually in different places, and we brought them all together on one platform at Teaneck armory. We'd have around 8,000 to 10,000 people praying at Teaneck armory, and around the same time we would be making arrangements for Iftar at the Marriott hotel with 500 to 600 people, inviting officials and other faiths. We invited the Jewish community, Christian community, and other communities to the Iftar to experience this.

M. Khateeb: Wow that sounds awesome, thank you for sharing that and some of the events you guys hold. So I'm going to get into something else I was curious about which was something you had already slightly mentioned. You mentioned you came from India to America so I'm wondering if anything inspired you to say "Hey we need an Eid Committee here in New Jersey" you know, and I also wanted to know that when you had this idea in 2004 and you started this, was it recognized amongst the communities living here? Were people noticing there's this committee that was forming, or was it just disregarded?

K. Khateeb: As you know, for Muslims, Eid is a major major holiday back in our countries, I mean there are two Eids, Eid al-Fitr and Eid al-Adha, so we thought it would be a good idea to celebrate Eid together and to bring all the different sectors of Islam together and bring unity amongst us. So we spoke to the mosques and had a lot of meetings back and forth, and finally, we formed the committee and started to make arrangements.

M. Khateeb: Right, that sounds like a lot of effort was put into that, that's crazy. So like I mentioned before when the Eid committee was created, how did you gain recognition, was it not easily brought up, how did you guys become big?

K. Khateeb: Our arrangements were getting really popular, so we would go to the Teaneck armory the night before and make all these arrangements with a nice beautiful ambiance, place the prayer mats, have beautiful decorations, and on the Eid day we would give out toys to the kids and a lot of sweets, even food sometimes. This is how we got popular, by making such beautiful arrangements and giving goodies to families.

M. Khateeb: That is sweet and something special for these families to get on Eid day. But, you just mentioned kids, and I will get right back to that as I point out that I've done my research, and it's safe to say, like you stated, that thousands of people attend these prayers, do you think a significant amount of those attending were kids?

K. Khateeb: Yes of course, because when it's a prayer, the whole family will come, and definitely when each family comes with 2 to 3 kids, there are a good amount of kids.

M. Khateeb: Yeah I would say if families are bringing their kids, that'll be a lot for sure, but again, I want to mention the sort of detriment those students are put at, and I'm going to refer to myself here and how I could go to these prayers because I'd go to school the day before and hand my teacher a note that reads "Dear Administrator, my daughter has a religious holiday tomorrow called Eid" from my mom, and I'd have to actually notify them you know. So I wanna know, if Eid was a national holiday, do you think more kids would be showing up to these prayers?

K. Khateeb: Definitely, I mean that'll make a big difference because I'd see sometimes some kids can't make it to the prayers because they'll realize they have a test or an exam on that day so if we already have a holiday in advance, kids will be able to pray. But now, we're not sure, maybe they'll have an exam or test on that day and that definitely makes kids, or students, miss the Eid prayer.

M. Khateeb: For sure, I agree.

K. Khateeb: So if we have a holiday, we will definitely have a much bigger gathering and the best part will be the kids accompanying their parents and celebrating Eid, which is the most important thing. The kids will miss their families who are out and enjoying at the armory or MetLife if they stay in school and that's just unacceptable. There are some towns, like New York state, where there is a holiday for Eid, but not New Jersey. So if every state makes it a holiday for at least Eid al-Fitr, if not for both Eids, the kids will enjoy their celebration with their families.

M. Khateeb: So this brings us to my next point, where these students that are missing Eid celebration and prayer really matter because these are still students that are having to choose between their education or school over their faith. These are kids that are believing they can't do anything for their religious holiday because they have to take a test or exam. Essentially, it's important for these kids to be seen. This brings me to my next point where there are schools that don't give a day off for Eid and Muslim students will feel inferior for not having their own holiday recognized. So other than having students choose over their education and faith, there are students who are completely unseen, unheard, and unrepresented when their holiday isn't being noticed as a national holiday. And when you look a the bigger picture you see Christianity and

THE DETRIMENT OF EID NOT BEING ACKNOWLEDGED AS A SCHOOL HOLIDAY

Judaism which have Christmas off, which is multiple days, and Rosh Hashanah off, so it really raises the question of what makes it so hard for our one Muslim holiday as a day off. So I wanted to see what you thought, what makes it so hard for one Muslim holiday to be recognized?

K. Khateeb: I mean it takes time, if you see, as I said before, there are states and towns that have announced Eid al-Fitr and Eid al-Adha, so eventually it comes down to awareness where Muslim leaders need to sit down with local officials, or local board of education members and explain to them what are these holidays and how important these holidays are to these kids and eventually it'll happen you know.

M. Khateeb: Yeah this definitely comes down to a strength of numbers kind of thing where our community needs to come together.

K. Khateeb: Our community is growing for sure, so I think as you said, when we can have Jewish and Christian holidays, we need to push out the question of why can't we have Eid off as well.

M. Khateeb: We definitely need to unite and fight together against this cause, because as you mentioned, we are growing as a community so if there's more of us, that's more of us to come together and fight for this cause. So what do you think the next step is to get Eid recognized as a national holiday?

K. Khateeb: We need to sit down, as I said, with officials, congressmen, and senators, and educate them on why this holiday is so important in Islam. This is how we can work on it and make it happen in a few years.

M. Khateeb: Do you think there are any smaller steps we can take, for example, signing petitions?

K. Khateeb: Signing petitions have already been done that I've seen, but obviously we can still do it. But I do think the best thing we can do is talk to our local members and leaders in the community and help them reach out to officials and explain to them that this is what we need. I mean listen, 10 years ago, have you heard of any town or state having Eid as a holiday? No. But now we have New York, and Teaneck (a town in New Jersey), that are giving off for Eid, so this is how it all starts, this is the beginning and eventually, it'll all happen.

M. Khateeb: These small steps are definitely making a difference, it's like a ripple or domino effect where you knock one over and the rest will follow, and it really comes back to how we are a minority now but that doesn't mean we stop fighting to make a difference

K. Khateeb: At the same time, when we prayed at MetLife stadium, it was all over social media, TV, ABC, Channel 7, CNN, it was everywhere, it was big national news. People were like "Wow 50,000 people prayed at MetLife, how did they get there?" Because it was Sunday. That's why. You have to understand that if it was a weekday, not that many people would've shown up

because of jobs, and as we do, if some kids have to go to school they will go to school, so just because it was a Sunday, so many people were able to show up.

M. Khateeb: Hundred percent, that really makes sense and I agree with you. And giving a day off will give them no option or choice to decide between school or faith.

K. Khateeb: As an organizer, when Eid falls on the weekends, we just make more arrangements because we know that more people will be there in comparison to the weekdays, at least 30% more.

M. Khateeb: I definitely agree, we need to make it so it's not a choice but rather a reality where a student can safely say they have off and can attend Eid prayer and we need to do that by coming together as a community and fighting for this and I think that's really important so Muslim students won't feel like they are in debt to go to school, come back and work twice as hard, whatever the case is, I think the solution is all of us coming together and fighting for the fact that Eid needs to be a national holiday. And that pretty much concludes what I wanted to discuss with you, is there anything you wanted to add?

K. Khateeb: No but thank you so much for interviewing me and I hope very soon we're going to have a national holiday for Eid

M. Khateeb: Agreed, thank you for the opportunity!

FULL 180

A Personal Account by Mehreen Khateeb

Ew, Eid.

I know, I know, it's quite the double negative. Eid, a holiday of unity and happiness, paired with a face of disgust. Let me explain…

Every year was the same. I walked up to my teachers with a note in hand and silently slid the note across their respective maple desks.

"Oh, you won't be in school tomorrow for, uh, how do I pronounce this?"

Gosh. I remember just how infuriated I'd be with the teachers; I mean, how hard can it be? It's three letters in the English alphabet, but somehow it's harder to pronounce than Christmas or Rosh Hashanah. Alas, I didn't correct them. Later, I adopted their Americanized pronunciation of Eid myself.

When it came to times like this, it often made me wonder how my life would be if I didn't celebrate Eid. Nobody would ask me where I was on the day of Eid, and instead, I'd get questions asking what I did for Christmas and what my parents bought me. Why couldn't I just be like everyone else?

Funnily enough, I formed a pretty intricate excuse system in the database of my elementary school brain.

"Hey, where were you yesterday? You didn't come to school," my friends would ask. "Haha, yeah, I wasn't feeling too good, so I stayed home," I'd reply.

I know. What a fraud. But can you blame me? The endless cycle of questions would begin if I told them I was celebrating Eid. Questions like, "Eid? What's that?" or "Wait, so this is because you didn't eat for 30 days straight… Wow. I could never."

Uh, yeah, Maddy, I could never either; I'd literally be dead. My sharp dialogue always stayed within my brain. In person, I would simply go along with their misinterpretations of Islam. "Yeah, it's really hard. I prevailed, though," I would reply.

So, I came to the conclusion that if being different was hard, I'd assimilate and be one of them, and it really came in clutch during Christmas time. During the holidays, the number one question coming out of everyone's mouth revolved around what everyone wanted. I guess it never occurred to me that maybe there were people out there who just didn't celebrate Christmas because, oh, I don't know, not everyone in the world was Christian, but you know me by now. I had to quickly reply, "I'm going Christmas shopping with my mom!"

Yeah right. The only Christmas shopping I'd be doing with my mom is taking advantage of the Christmas sales at TJ Maxx.

The excuses only became more elaborate over time. Picture this: I'm in the 2nd grade, in the thick of springtime, and Eid is stealthily approaching.

Just like I said before, I'd come in with my note stating I wouldn't be in school the following day, and per usual, the teacher, aloud, converses with me on how interesting this was and how she wished I had fun. Due to her extreme loudness, my friend overheard and was obviously curious. Now I couldn't pull a fast one and use the sick excuse. After all, what kind of kid can predict they'll be sick and hand in a note a day in advance for it? No one! Right? Wrong. While my friend was pressuring me into exposing why I wasn't coming to school the next day, I was coming up with the most believable story out there.

"I'm sick."

"You don't look sick."

"That's because"—I inch closer to my friend—"it's a non-noticeable issue that's slowly affecting me on the inside."

"Like an ulcer?"

"Uh-yeah, exactly."

Now, clearly, I didn't know where I was going with this because there was no way she would catch me 'lackin'' and find out I was absent for Eid. Anyways, frankly, I returned the day after and pulled off a little "Yeah, I got cured" to her, and all ended well, but that's not the point. The big picture here is how silly I was. I mean, really? Faking an illness, come on now! So, yeah, I was quite a unique child, but even now, sometimes I wouldn't even blame my younger self. I remember feeling so unseen and unheard because my experiences talking about Eid often ended up going down the same path of many people raising eyebrows and facial wrinkles of confusion. Essentially, I was ignored. I say this because I never drove past a house to see a "Happy Eid" or "Eid Mubarak" sign like you'd see for Christmas. I never heard a teacher say, "We won't be in school tomorrow," like you'd hear for Rosh Hashanah. I simply never experienced a time where I, as a minority, was recognized.

I think I started having a change of heart when I heard the issue coming out of the mouth of people I admired. My uncles, cousins, and parents all had something to say about it. Hearing the pure words of compassion made me realize that what I had been going through all along was wrong, and I wasn't the only kid who went through it. I vividly recall my cousin talking about the injustice she faced in school because of the henna that lay on her hands. Henna was part of my culture, and many applied such beautiful and intricate designs to celebrate Eid, so why was my cousin shamed for it? I felt disgusted. Why didn't anybody know what Eid was, and why didn't I appreciate it? I realized that the more I

EQUAL OPPURTUNITY

covered up about it, the more other people would be unaware of such a religious holiday, and right now, my mission, just like my family's and many others, should be getting more people to know exactly why I'm out that one day in the school year.

If I had to talk about my progress from then to now, I'd claim that there is, in fact, a lot of it. Now, I'm involved in letting everyone know what Eid is and when it is. Just last year, I was posting all over my social media on the special upcoming day. I would be getting so many likes and comments on my posts, with people from school wishing me a "Happy Eid," which would warm my heart. Occasionally, I'd have people, including teachers, hit me with the "So what do you do on Eid?" But at this point, I don't look at it with any negativity, and instead, as a way to have people learn about Eid and the happiness it brings to my community. If anything, I would love for more people to show their interest and appreciation for my faith because that just gives more opportunities for me to explain the peace and love my religion shares. I hope many people

in my community we have a wake-up call that we're a minority that is constantly overlooked, and whenever we are given attention, it's for the wrong reasons. Because of this, many aren't willing to look into Eid and find out what it's about. Aside from the wrong reasons, again, this is just an issue of lack of awareness. Just because we don't parade through the streets on fire trucks and floats doesn't mean there aren't other ways to make our holiday known. As I mentioned before, the joy I now feel from teaching others and posting about it is something I know others can feel if they do the same.

Now, I sit on a board that helps advocate for Muslim issues, one reaching into Eid attendance policies and the central concept of lack of awareness. My friends are reaching out to me on how they can join because they want to help join the fight for our community, and it's amazing to see. We need to use our voices to make a change, and that change is one step closer for the younger generations to not be like how I was, to not be embarrassed, and to not be dishonest. We all need to be proud of who we are and what we celebrate.

Past all my endeavors, the day I'm looking forward to the most this year is Eid. I know, full 180.

Chapter 4:

The Negative Effects of the Flawed P.E. System Towards Muslim Students

THE NEGATIVE EFFECTS OF THE FLAWED P.E. AND SPORTS SYSTEM TOWARDS MUSLIM STUDENTS

By Mateen Aminyar

Throughout all school subjects, which one would you choose as the most challenging? At first, the answer might seem straightforward: a core subject, such as math, English, history, or science. The answers vary so much that a subject that some students seem to look forward to can be a nightmare to many others. With this in mind, physical education has been seen by a majority of kids as the best subject. However, it can be hell for many Muslims in oppressive school systems. Further, certain education systems can bring about a certain hatred or suffering because of their policies that work out of favor for Muslims. To start, the main grievance for Muslim students partaking in physical education is the detriment fasting gives them since they can't eat or drink during the exercises. Furthermore, the physical education dress codes have forced many women into dreading having to perform any physical activity, as they do not consider Islamic restrictions regarding skin coverings. Both of these can also be applied in extracurricular sports programs in schools, whether having to take a break during practices or a game because of fasting or not being able to wear the required attire for the practices or games. To put the cherry on top, Muslims are faced with a repeated struggle: the choice of their religion or education. Additionally, despite

EQUAL OPPURTUNITY

going hungry, Muslims are not excused from skipping gym or sports. With this in mind, it becomes clear that a universal compromise must be made to allow Muslims to have equal opportunity in both physical education and sports. The core problem here isn't just physical education or sports but equality for all students, allowing every student to be given the same opportunities. With this, the all-encompassing theme of these grievances is that there is a dire need for sports and physical education policy reform in schools for the sake of our Muslim student population.

Fasting is one of the most important principles in Islam, a religious experience Muslims look forward to. Fasting periods occur on the 9th month of the Islamic lunar calendar and typically span 30 days. Having to abstain from food and drink from dusk till dawn evokes a sense of empathy in Muslims and helps them understand the lives of the less fortunate. As one of the five core pillars of Islam, it is of complete importance that you recognize this tradition for the sake of faith. With this in mind, physical effort during fasting inevitably causes a huge burden on Muslims, as they can not replenish the energy they lose through exercise. This puts Muslims at a huge disadvantage in areas like physical education or their sports team. In many cases, one's level of ability in physical education determines their grade in the class. However, because Muslims are depleted of vital energy, they can not perform certain tasks to the best of their abilities, leading to worse grades and straining students academically for something simply out of their control. Moreover, many athletes rely on their performance to attain their starting spot in a lineup. Other sports require full attendance to keep one's spot on a sports team/lineup. Sports are a valuable extracurricular and a point of passion for many students. For Muslims to face easily avoidable injustices is completely and utterly unacceptable. With all of this in mind, one might believe that there must be some compromise within Islam to suit these children, such as skipping fasting to perform better. However, according to Sheikh Kifah Mustapha, "missing fasting for such reasons is not acceptable at all," and they must "make up for all the days he missed" (Council of Islamic Organizations of Greater Chicago). These conflicting areas bring about much controversy and spark the valid question: Why has there been no effort for schools to rectify these clear disparities?

Before we get to the best course of action, we must expand on the other conflicting aspect of physical effort and Islam: the dress code. According to the Islamic faith, "Some Muslim women wear full-body garments that only expose the eyes, although there is no Quranic text requiring this extreme. Some cover every part of the body except their face and hands. Some believe only their hair or their cleavage is compulsory to hide"(Cornell University). Even if children are willing to abide by the intense restrictions Islam requires for women, they get put in a consistently awkward position during physical activities at school. Having said that, many schools require dress codes for physical activities. These dress codes can range from having athletic shoes on to not being able to wear long-sleeved shirts or long pants, which is the most common form of attire for Muslim women. With this in mind, wearing such tight and multiple amounts of clothing causes Muslim women to sweat profoundly, making them uncomfortable and unable to perform at their best in physical education, or rather not even wanting to perform in anticipation of this discomfort. This doesn't only happen in physical education, however. These dress code rules can also be seen in an array of sports teams, where the typical uniform archetype entails short-sleeved shirts and shorts. By forcing Muslim women to wear this, it prohibits them from joining certain sports for fear of deciding between faith or sports since they must wear covering clothes. To continue, even if the dress codes weren't that important, coaches wouldn't prefer someone who would go against the dress code that everyone else follows (even if it isn't strictly put into place), leading to an even bigger disadvantage for Muslim women who want to join a team. The bigger picture with dress codes is that they restrict Muslim women from partaking in sports. All in all, it's clear that sports and gym dress codes are simply not taking into account Islamic dress codes nor leaving leeway for compromise.

These problems must be addressed as soon as possible so all Muslims are given fair representation. District-wide policies need to be enacted to excuse fasting students from sports meets or gym classes if they are not fit to partake. Further, students should not be punished or face any detriment for these uncontrollable grievances. Or, they could even allow the students to take breaks whenever they feel it necessary to perform at their best. The solution doesn't have to be a cut-and-dry answer, but just bringing attention to it will allow coaches to become more understanding about Muslim problems and allow them to take their own initiative on it. Coaches should understand that choosing between faith and sports is a terrible position to put any student in and that fasting is something Muslims must comply with. The next problem that needs to be fixed is dress coding. The solution to this is very simple; schools should just amend their policies to allow Muslims to follow their faith while still being within school guidelines. This means allowing them to wear however much clothing they need without being forced to change. This is not to say that all dressing is allowed. It just means that for the requirements that Muslims need in terms of clothing, which means the ability to cover body parts, is met by the dress code. This can be done through a special rule for Muslims or by just bringing a broader policy to the board for all students, allowing even non-Muslims to benefit from this rule by being allowed to cover up if they don't feel comfortable. By adding solutions like these to the education system,

Muslims will transition from an uneven ground to a level playing field.

All in all, the several physical activity-related grievances Muslim students face are the sole evidence of the urgent need for reform. All students in the education system are the future, and none should be disadvantaged. Equal rights lead to equal opportunity while also promoting diversity and inclusion. With this in mind, what should be done is not create an uneven distribution of opportunity and advantages. What should be done is not give Muslims advantages over other students but rather allow them to be the same as everyone else in terms of education and sports possibilities. Imagine a world where everyone was given an equal chance, from sports to academics, and finally, how a community treats one another. If a certain group is oppressed, people will treat it differently. Therefore, if Muslims are given the same rights as everyone else in terms of fasting with sports and dress codes, they will be treated by society equally since that's the rights they are given. So, if schools were to enact several policies that tend to the needs of Muslims around the world, American schools would be a much better place for all and would truly follow the idea of equal representation and opportunity for all.

INTERVIEW WITH AHMET GUNDOGDU, 12TH GRADE STUDENT AND VARSITY TENNIS PLAYER

Interview conducted by Mateen Aminyar

Aminyar: Hi Ahmet! How are you?

Gundogdu: I'm great! So thankful to be meeting today discussing injustice.

Aminyar: Yeah! I'd like to once again express my gratitude in you meeting with me and discussing your struggles as a Muslim student-athlete.

Gundogdu: Absolutely, and I'd love to go more in-depth for your readers!

Aminyar: For sure. Just as a quick reminder, We at the Muslim Students for Justice Organization, a nonprofit organization I sit on the board of, are trying to fight Muslim Injustice. My particular subject of study is sports, and the challenges Muslim students face when playing them. Being a student-athlete myself, I have a great deal of negative experiences regarding playing sports while fasting. More particularly, I had a lot of issues regarding exemptions and break times with my coaches, who were perhaps not so aware of the fasting regiment we partake in during

Ramadan. Since you played sports during Ramadan as well, why don't you go over some of the struggles you've faced?

Gundogdu: Yeah, so the past few years, the spring tennis season has overlapped with Ramadan. As you said, it's not easy to play your sport on an empty stomach. Not to mention I had to go through 7 hours of school without water and food, which would only take a further toll on me. With that, I really have a passion for tennis, so I was willing to put up the strenuous effort. I particularly remember my coach informing me that I wasn't playing at my best and my efforts were rather weak. I really do think this is one of the issues at hand. Because members of administration are not made aware of fasting periods and Muslim holidays, they express rather problematic sentiments about their Muslim players, not knowing that they are struggling. I really do think that Muslims should be able to get the best of both worlds. Maybe they won't play at their complete best, but they should still be allowed to be a part of the team without facing disadvantage due to their situation.

Aminyar: What do you think your peers and coaches could have done to make fasting a better experience for you?

Gundogdu: There isn't anything specific that the teammates can do besides understand and respect Islam. As for the coaches, I think that their strict attendance policies could use some edits. I remember last year, I had to take a leave from the tennis team. I missed a game due to starvation/exhaustion. I missed about a week of practice. According to my coach's attendance policy, missing a week of practice and games resulted in me being banned from the next week of tennis. I felt a sense of rage that I was being forced to pick between my religion and faith, and I felt really misunderstood.

Aminyar: I agree with that, and do you agree that it is the coaches responsible for their naivety of Islam, or do you think that it is a Board of Education policy problem?

Gundogdu: I don't think the Board is trying to target Muslim students but that they just can't comprehend the Muslim faith as well as being naive about it. They create a broad sports policy, but each coach adds edits. With that, I do think the board of education is responsible for making a universal rule that students should face no penalty for missing practice if it is fasting-related. They don't understand that Muslims can't drink or eat, so creating a sense of awareness is really the first step.

Aminyar: Right, and I think it's so important because this issue doesn't only apply to you. In fact, I think the issue will only grow as more Muslims pop up in the school district.

Gundogdu: Absolutely. Actually, during Ramadan, I noticed other Muslims fasting during gym class. Particularly, I remember an argument breaking out between a gym teacher and a Muslim student. The gym teacher was mad at the student for not participating in gym class and even gave her a 0 for her class participation. This is just one of a plethora of examples of Muslims being put at an educational detriment due to something they can't control, their faith. No student should pick between fasting and school, and no one should have their grades suffer due to this. I really did like how that student stood up for herself; it's especially hard when we feel so ignored as a community.

Aminyar: Absolutely. With that, what do you think would be the best policy enacted into the district sports handbook?

Gundogdu: Going into the season, coaches have expectations of the players, like attending practices, games, and training. I think what the change can really touch upon is to give flexibility to Muslim students for fasting. I want people to understand that this is extremely important to us, and we can't give this up. After I returned from my banishment from the tennis team, the least I expected was for my spot on the lineup to still be there. After all, I already did my punishment, I couldn't imagine being punished further upon my return. However, this wasn't the case. I was demoted from the 3rd highest position on the team to one of the lowest positions, on Junior varsity at that. Not only was tennis so important to me, but I really wanted to use that as a focal point of my college applications. In the end, I had to throw that away. To colleges, it actually looks bad because it looks as though I was demoted from varsity to junior varsity for a talent reason when it was really just because of my religion. Due to this, I think that schools nationwide should enact fasting policies that won't put students at any detriment if they need to take a break from their sport, and there can be no negative sentiment expressed towards them.

Aminyar: I think it is important for them to be understanding, as we aren't asking a lot from the coaches besides being accepting or understanding. With that in mind, did you ever feel at a crossroads between your faith and sport, and if so, what did you end up choosing?

Gundogdu: I think so. Because I had to take a leave due to me fasting, I ended up having to pick my faith. This is not to say I ever felt that I should just take that sip of water or eat that protein bar. It was definitely an urge, which only evokes more guilt in one as a person. So really, the only fix would be for school administration to step in.

Aminyar: Definitely, I think taking action is one of the most important things to do, and have you spoken to anyone or know any ideas that should be done to take action against this injustice?

Gundogdu: Yeah. I actually took this matter to the athletic director but was mortified to not even get an ounce of acceptance there, either. Truly, I felt rather alone and isolated.

Aminyar: Wow. I'm so sorry you felt this way and hope that with us creating more awareness, we can solidify a future of equality for the future Muslim students of America. I thank you for your time today and commend you in being so raw with your experiences and truly taking these injustices like a class act.

Gundogdu: No, thank you. I really appreciate what you guys are doing and am excited to see the change.

REFORM, NEVER TOLERATE

A Short Story By Mateen Aminyar

When I was younger, I hated my life.

It sounds like an exaggeration, but I felt life couldn't get any worse. Not only was I moving constantly from Queens to Teaneck, from Teaneck to Hackensack, and from Hackensack to Paramus, but I faced so much discrimination wherever I went for my faith: Islam.

By no means was I an extremely religious child. But, I still learned to pray, fast, read the Quran, and follow Islamic principles and beliefs. I had grown to love my faith and the Muslim community. As a kid, though, my opinions were only contingent on what my friends and peers thought. It's important to know that bigotry is learned not inherent, and this was the perfect example.

All the kids in my school made jokes about Muslims, so it was hard for me to speak about my faith or connect with anyone. Being a new kid made it hard to make friends, but fighting stereotypes on top of that made it impossible for me to survive the school environment. In fact, I was too nervous to even tell people about my heritage, as I am from Afghanistan. We would learn about the horrific Afghanistan War in history and read first-hand accounts of those affected by Islamic terrorism in English class. Due to this, I would always tell people I was German. As time went on, I learned it was way easier to battle injustices silently rather than try to make a change. Besides, who would listen to a Muslim kid?

Fast forward a few years to the Covid-19 pandemic. Online school was great for me. I had so much extra time to dedicate to my true passion: sports. I became engrossed with basketball and track; I practiced every day so that I could become better once the season came along.

Eventually, I became a freshman in high school and was ready to join the basketball and track teams. I loved basketball, but I was always judged as a bad player because I didn't fight the typical "basketball player" stereotype. In truth, I was often hit with the, "What, no way you're Muslim!", after I would perform well.

Though it was meant as a compliment, these types of comments made me very agitated, as I knew many Muslims that were good at basketball, so there should be no correlation between being Muslim and being athletic. To continue, even on the court, I would hear a lot of trash talk about my religion, but I learned to endure it and just let my game do the talking. Even though it was rough, I was able to get through basketball season with my pride as a Muslim still intact.

However, spring soon came, which meant track and Ramadan. Ramadan is a 30-day Islamic holiday, where Muslims aren't allowed to eat or drink from sunrise to sundown. Many non-Muslims think this is a punishment, but it was a very important holiday for me. I was able to understand how much I take for granted and how there is always something to appreciate. With this in mind, I would never willingly give up on Ramadan, but I never noticed that Ramadan was during the spring track season. This conflicting schedule didn't seem like it would pose many problems, so when I signed up for track, I entered with a lot of enthusiasm and speed.

Once I joined track, I made sure to do short-distance, as I loved sprinting. With this in mind, I was very fast, and it seemed like I could become one of the best on the team. However, a month into the track season, Ramadan started. This meant I had to go through every practice and track meet without water or food. At first, I thought I could just miss a couple of days, and it would be no big deal, but I soon realized there was a penalty for missing a certain number of practices. My friend had joined track and missed some practice days for soccer, a valid excuse (as track coincided with other spring sports). However, even with that, he was eventually kicked out for missing too many practices. I became curious about what constituted an excused absence and what did not, so I asked around. I was shocked that fasting was not a valid excuse to miss practice. So, even if I got tired or fatigued, I was gonna have to pull through.

With this fear instilled in me, I became nervous about missing any practices, and since there were no other Muslims on the team, I couldn't relate to anyone or speak about my problems. They always say, "power in numbers." It's safe to say that, as a minority, I never had that luxury. Since I was the only Muslim on the team, the coaches would never understand what Muslims had to go through in Ramadan and the struggles that came with performing a sport. For the first two weeks of Ramadan, I fought through it and went to every practice and meet, running the best I could but still noticeably slower than before. Eventually, I was brought from the 1st seat to the 2nd and the 2nd to the 3rd. Fasting began affecting me physically, but by bringing down my seat, it also brought down my confidence. One time at a meet, we had a team competition where four people ran one lap each and tried competing against other schools. Since I was considered fast because of my tryout, I was moved to the anchor, the most important position since it gave me the opportunity to beat everybody in the last stretch. Once my teammate handed me the baton to go, I ran as fast as I could, and even though the person in front of me had half the lap done, I managed to catch up to him. However, in the last 50 meters of the race, I could feel my exhaustion from not drinking or eating, and I wanted to throw up and give up. I lost the race but got a new personal best. So, I was really happy, but the struggle of fasting and running gave me a sign of what was to come.

My final breaking point was at practice one day—a day so hot you could see the humidity on the field. We were running multiple laps at full speed, and I had to go my fastest otherwise, the coaches would drop me even further or even consider moving me down entirely. Although I managed to maintain my spot in that practice, by the time practice ended, I was severely drained of everything and got a heat stroke. My friend helped to carry me off the field as I was so exhausted I couldn't even think straight. Once I got home, I had to break my fast immediately, and that is when I realized I had to talk to my coaches about my fasting problems.

I talked to my coaches about my problems in the hope that they would understand. At first, some of the coaches didn't seem to really care or understand, and all they really cared about was results. Meaning if I didn't perform well or attend practices, it was on me. However, this changed when the head coach talked to me about fasting and my problems, and he allowed me to miss practice days or track meets a certain amount of days to ensure I gained my energy back while following my faith. This not only caused me to feel physically better but also psychologically. Running every day through the pain put me in a very bad spot, and I didn't want to let my team down. However, now that I was given the option to take time off, I could feel much better about myself and more healthy in general. I was able to end the season not feeling disappointed and just grateful for my coach.

These experiences led me to try and help other Muslims in their fight for sports equality. For most of my life, I was always too scared to try and make a change, but by fighting for my faith, I gained courage and learned that I don't have to sacrifice my faith for anything. With this in mind, I was able to join my friends in creating the nonprofit organization, The Muslim Students For Justice Organization. Since then, I have tried to institute a change in the sports policies affecting our school and others. Though we have started by speaking with the Paramus Board of Education, we will continue to fight for more sports equality for Muslims to give them a fairer opportunity since Muslims already face so much injustice and shouldn't have to go through even more in sports. In fact, I was instrumental in passing a district-wide policy declaring that an excused absence is mandatory to be given if a fasting student misses practice or needs a break due to fasting struggles.

I stick with a very clear motto now:

Reform, never tolerate.

Final Remarks

FINAL REMARKS

The Muslim Students For Justice Organization set out to prove the following: the United States public schooling system fails to accommodate for the Muslim-American student, creating a feeling of alienation for Muslim students everywhere. In this novel, essays, interviews, and personal accounts came together not just to prove the aforementioned statement, but to elevate the voices of the previously unheard and underrepresented Muslim students who face these issues.

The implications of these discrimination-based issues within the education system stretch far beyond the K-12 sphere. Facing alienation and having exposure to bias at such a young age can be detrimental for students, stifling their potential growth and successes as they deal with a crippling sense of estrangement. As schools prepare to send young minds into the American workforce to create new members of the U.S. economy, they will find that those students will become less engaged members of the workforce, leading to a lack of productivity and output.

Beyond the economic implications, religious discriminations and a lack of accommodation in schools creates disastrous implications for the mental health of those students affected. It perpetuates feelings of lonesomeness, which can stem into anxiety and depression. As mental health becomes a more pressing issue in the U.S. (with a huge rise in the percentage of population inflicted with mental health issues), it is a duty of the American school system to target and diminish any routes to poor mental health amongst students.

It is worthy to mention, however, that it is not enough to simply identify issues of Islamophobia within school systems and their implications. Work and effort must both be put in to pinpoint and diminish these issues, so that future generations do not have to endure the same alienation Muslim students have faced for many years. In a word, school systems must become more *accommodating*. In accommodating Muslim students and their faith, they would allow a higher quality of learning, as students would feel more welcome and understood as a minority group.

Education is the foundation for the path of young students lives in the United States. It is where they develop their personality, make their core childhood memories, find their future life's calling and career pathway, and develop both social and emotional intelligence. Creating a nurturing and welcoming environment for students is crucial in making sure that they succeed in finding these things and become functioning and flourishing constituents of the United States. Targeting and eradicating systemic Islamophobia and other religious discrimination from school systems is the first step in improving the U.S. education system and allowing for more representation, equality, and justice within America's youth, creating a better and brighter future for America's children.

ABOUT THE ORGANIZATION

At the Muslim Students for Justice Organization, we strive to eliminate Islamophobia in the American education system for good. In doing so, we've spread ourselves out to several different forms of multimedia and concepts to get our ideas across. For starters, we have Spotify podcast titles, "Critical Conversations on Muslim Injustice", in which we interview legislators, like Mayor Khairullah of Prospect Park and New York City Councilman Rafael Espinal. On the podcast, we interview legislators who somehow relate to what we focus on, Muslim injustice.

Moreover, we have our blog updated every week on our website, muslimstudentsforjustice.org. On our blog, we discuss new and happening events regarding Muslims that we hope inspire oppressed Muslim students to stand out! Most importantly, we have our policy work. In our policy work, we alter already existing policies, or just create new ones, to better the lives of

Muslim students. Recently, the organization passed two "Pro-Muslim" policies in Paramus, New

Jersey, in which Muslim students fasting during Ramadan can be excused from P.E. and After School Sports, and halal foods are now being served in school cafeterias. Lastly, we have our novel, *Equal Opportunity*. In the novel, we hope that this can be used as a guidebook for future Muslim students, and also push legislators and change makers alike to reform these pressing issues. As a 501(c)(3) non-profit organization, we will not be taking any profit from the book, but instead, injecting it back into our causes. All in all, we appreciate your support and hope you stay along for the ride.

Made in the USA
Middletown, DE
13 January 2023